The AWAKENED
Goddess Detox

A HEART-CENTERED GUIDE TO DETOXING BODY, MIND & SOUL, MASTERING SELF-LOVE, AND MANIFESTING THE HEALTHY LIFE YOU DESERVE

NATHALIE SADER

COPYRIGHT

Name: Awakened Goddess LLC
Address: 1413 Mayo Rd.
Edgewater, MD 21037

Website: **www.nathaliesader.com**

ISBN: 978-1-7350059-1-1 (Hard Cover)
ISBN: 978-1-7350059-9-7 (Paperback)
ISBN: 978-1-7350059-7-3 (Epub)
ISBN: 978-1-7350059-5-9 (Mobi)

DISCLAIMER

Nothing in this book should be considered as professional advice and is not intended to be used in this manner. All the content of this book is for informational purpose only and is not a substitute for professional nutritional or medical advice or treatment. Consult with your physician or qualified healthcare professional regarding the applicability of any information provided herein before beginning this detoxification or any exercise, nutritional, weight loss, or health care regimen.

Dedication

This book is a tribute to all the women who are being called to break free from anything that is no longer serving them and to create a new paradigm in their relationship with food, their body and their mind.

I see you, I feel you, I acknowledge you. I am you.

Thank you for inspiring me without even knowing it.

Love and grace,

Nathalie

Endorsements

"This book will awaken all your senses. This beautiful goddess Nathalie has found just the right words and style to impart important life lessons. It's like having a chat with your wisest friend who reminds you how best to take care of your body, mind and soul and live a healthy happy life. *The Awakened Goddess Detox* is a book ALL women should read."

Mimi Kirk
Best selling author, of 7 books, inspirational speaker

"If you know Nathalie, you know that she does everything with her complete heart and Soul. Nathalie is empowering women (and men) to liberate themselves from archaic ideologies that have been holding them back from loving themselves completely. Her method to physical, mental, and emotional well-being is special and offers a whole view approach that feels like a best friend is right there with you championing you every step of the way. If you are ready to receive support in a way that will nourish, inspire, and uplift you in extraordinary ways, do yourself a big favor and get to know Nathalie Sader's work, and gift yourself and your loved ones with her new book *The Awakened Goddess Detox*!"

Emmanuel Dagher
Spiritual teacher, healer, and bestselling author

Table of Contents

Introduction

I got a phone call from my best friend Maya in Lebanon not too long ago. It was passed midnight here in the US and I had forgotten to switch my phone to airplane mode, so I answered half-asleep with a mumbled hello.

> *"It's working! It's working!" she said excitedly.*
>
> *I guessed what she was talking about, but I still hoped she was not waking me up in the middle of the night to tell me about another diet!*
>
> *So I said, "What's working? What are you talking about?"*
>
> *"The detox. I lost five pounds and I'm only on Day 5! Can you believe it? Oh wait, are you sleeping? Oh n-o-o-o-o, I am so sorry, talk tomorrow, I will send you a picture in my new jeans, love ya."*

For as long as I can remember, Maya has been chasing the perfect body, I can't count how many diets she's been on, how many detoxes she's gone through. From Paleo and Dr. Atkins to intermittent fasting, liver flushes and back, I have witnessed it all and even participated in a few.

Three weeks after Maya completed the 10-day juice detox, she had regained the weight and slumped into a depression—and thrown the jeans in the bottom drawer where she wouldn't be reminded of yet another failure. Actually, she had tried to extend her detox because she didn't want to lose that "high" or gain the weight she'd lost but she was only able to do it for two and a half more days before she caved. She was starving and feeling miserably in control! Within a week, she slipped back into her old way of eating which consisted of a continuous war between binging on processed and fast food and depriving herself until starvation.

There are lots of reasons people start detox programs: to improve their sluggish digestive process, boost their energy, or get rid of environmental toxins, among others. But most people see it as a way to drop pounds rapidly. As a health coach with a background in clinical psychology, that's usually the starting point for the women that come to me. Their primary goal is to lose the weight that is keeping them (they believe) from being happy and achieving their dreams.

The common refrain is: "If only I had a perfect, beautiful body, then my life would be perfect too." Everything else would fall into place, their relationship, their career, their happiness would be secured. This is a pervasive, destructive myth promoted by media, advertisers, and so-called diet and health gurus. It's also the reason I wrote this book which is to expose this myth for what it is and to offer a different perspective that frees women from this painful merry-go-round.

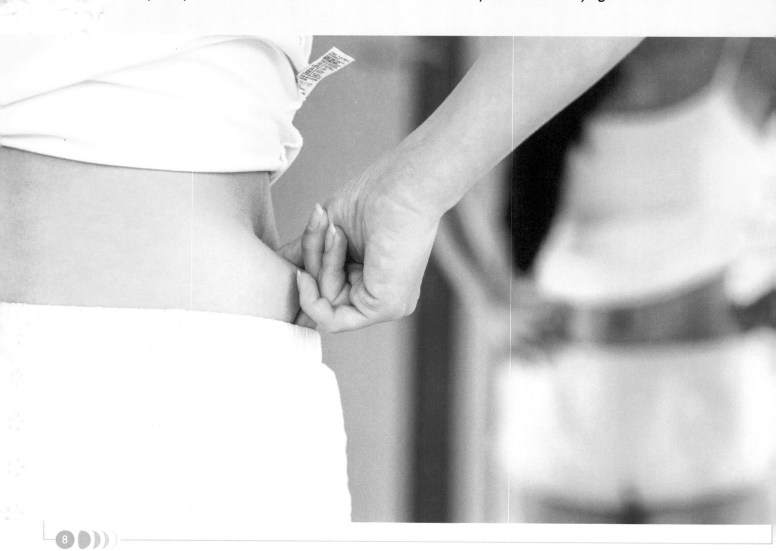

My Story

When I first tried to solve my problems by changing my lifestyle, like most people, I started with food—not because I didn't know there was more to deal with but because food seemed less painful. Since I had moved to the U.S. from my beautiful home country of Lebanon, I was no longer eating the wonderful, healthful meals my mother cooked for the family. Instead, my husband and I were eating out in restaurants nearly every night. I had left my clinical practice, I didn't know the language or the culture. Faced with this major life change, I was experiencing chaos and upheaval on every level of my being— physical, mental and emotional. It was an exciting but stressful time that played havoc with my health and state of mind. I drastically changed my diet to try to work with the situation.

For over two years I followed a strict macrobiotic diet, which consisted mostly of brown rice, vegetables, beans, and occasional white fish. When I first began to lose weight, it was exhilarating. As the pounds rolled off, I loved the feeling of being in control. Finally, I was in charge and not food. Food was not going to take me down. I had conquered it! This exhilaration and initial sense of power did not last long, however. Soon I felt deprived. When friends saw me refusing to take a serving of potatoes (the dreaded member of the "nightshades" family, along with tomatoes and eggplant), they often complimented me. "Oh, I wish I had your discipline!" I would smile smugly but inside I was miserable.

Forbidden food was the culprit, lurking at every turn so I had to stay guarded and prepare for the attack. On the few occasions when I caved in and ate a piece of fruit, I worried whether or not I was going to get sick because it was too yin, which was one of the dogmatic claims of the macrobiotic system. I became too thin, gaining only ten pounds during pregnancy which may sound like a dream to a lot of women including myself, and it was nice but at what price? I was eating "clean" and I was perversely proud of that fact when I compared myself to other "unfortunates" who were not. However, I lived in fear of losing control and I became too rigid not only in my appearance but also in my thinking--intolerant, dogmatic with little compassion in my heart!

Food Is Not the Enemy

Slowly I began to realize that I had made food THE enemy. I became aware that the thoughts in my head about food were mostly negative and prescriptive. I was obsessed. What should I eat, what should I not eat, when and how much should I eat? I was in a battle with the very substance provided by the bounteous earth that was meant to nourish me! It was exhausting and so limiting.

Most detox and diet programs focus solely on food for losing weight and improving our health as their primary goals. The reason I believe so many people experience failure is that they begin from the wrong end. The impact of the food you eat is a small element compared with what's going on in your mind! You could be sitting there eating the healthiest meal on the planet, and if you are angry or disturbed or thinking negative thoughts, it will not benefit you—it may even harm you (more on that later). The invisible enemy behind our "failure" is negative self- talk—those harsh self-condemning judgments that often plague our thinking and undermine our efforts.

No matter what I do, I am never going to have the body I want.

I am such a loser, I have no discipline.

The food always wins no matter what I do.

Whatever I eat doesn't make any difference because nothing really works for me.

I'm a hopeless case, what am I going to do now?

When you try and don't get the results you want time after time, like Maya, you create a cycle that's easy to get stuck in. You may not even be aware of the mean and unkind things you are telling yourself, things you would never to say to your friends! I know that feeling of being overwhelmed when you just keep repeating the cycle and it feels like there's nothing you can do to break it. That your habits are just too strong to overcome. I understand how exhausting it may feel to have to deal with this every single day of your life! Meanwhile, as this painful cycle keeps repeating itself, you may finally say, "I'll just eat whatever I want to fill that void so maybe I can numb this feeling of failure."

I hear you, I feel you and I am here to tell there is a way out, a way for you to regain control, but perhaps not in the way you think or imagine.

My Detoxification Program

My 3-part Detoxification Program is designed to replace your struggle with food and weight, not with deprivation, but with the ease and pleasure of true nourishment at all levels of your being—body, mind, and spirit. Parts One and Two guide you with inspiration, tools and rituals to connect with your inner wisdom as an awakened goddess and let go of deprivation and self-punishment. Leads you to understand and use the transformative power of thought and emotion to achieve your goals. And finally, to embrace self-love, self-care and the bounty of earth's amazing gifts. This is our heritage.

In Part Three, you're going on a **7-Day Detox Adventure** designed to allow your body and mind to make an *enjoyable* shift to transform your eating habits. You'll learn recipes that will inspire you to create your own in the future by mixing and matching meals that will *support* the change you want. What you'll notice right away when you look at the 7-day protocol is that this approach is not extreme. There are no fasts, rigid juice detoxes, or extremely narrow food choices. Instead, what you will find here is a generous variety of plant-based foods and menus to wake up your taste buds and give you energy.

Here's what you can expect to learn and experience while going through the program.

- *How to detox from your dysfunctional relationship with food*

- *The easy (and enjoyable!) way to transform your eating habits*

- *Why (and how) to approach food from a vibrational point of view*

- *Why negative thoughts keep you from losing weight*

- *How visualization and other rituals can help you achieve the body you want*

- *How to stop negative self-talk from running your life*

- *How mirror dance and positive affirmations can help you let go of resistance*

- *Why detoxing old beliefs is the key to your success*

- *How to unconditionally love and accept yourself by awakening your inner goddess*

- *Why pleasure (not pain) will get you there*

- *Why trusting your body is the key (the basis of this work)*

We live in a culture today that has normalized the obsession with dieting and weight loss. Everyone is on the alert for the next diet, food craze or study that offers a new protocol or warns of the dangers of certain foods. Experts sprout up everywhere fanatically prescribing what we should eat and what we should not eat so that we may be spared the ravages of cancer, Alzheimer's, ulcers, obesity, heart disease—you name it. We are now more than ever scared and obsessed, about the food we eat, confusing our bodies, and lost between contradictory beliefs that are constantly changing and a reality that feels stuck and desperate. There is another way that is based on joy and I invite you to try it. What have you got to lose?

Part I

CREATE YOUR BEAUTIFUL
BODY (AND LIFE)

Chapter One

THE MYTH OF DIETING
Why Your Diets Don't Work

After I got off the phone with Maya that night, I hoped and even prayed that she had found THE solution even though I knew deep down, it was just another fad.

So what's the real problem here? Why does diet after diet never work for Maya, for you, and for millions of others whose desire to have a beautiful body that they love is sincere and totally committed?

The problem is not the diet itself, it is its sustainability.

The High

When you begin a program *just for weight loss*, whether a diet or detox protocol, it's exciting—and new. You feel hopeful. You believe that this time it's going to work and often in the beginning it does because belief is powerful. You watch the numbers on the scale go down and it creates a high, a sense of control which feels really good. At last, you're doing it! Two pounds, then five, then at some point, in a week or a month, it stops working. Even if you are still losing weight, the high begins to fade then disappear, replaced by disappointment, frustration or just plain boredom.

Why? Because dieting is so restricting, physically and mentally—it dampens your spirit and tends to isolate you socially. You are also depriving yourself and when we deprive ourselves, we are going against our nature and we eventually rebel against that. We lose our faith in it. Let's say you believe in something so strong, but as days go by, you notice that even though you are a supporter and a huge fan of that belief, it's not making you feel good, and despite your will power, you find yourself drifting away from it. This is your intrapersonal intelligence at work.

I like to compare a new diet to a new lover—oh, the charm of new beginnings, can anyone relate here? At first, we don't see our new love as they really are but the way we want to see them. Little by little, as we get to know the person, the feeling of exhilaration fades, not necessarily because the person has changed but because of two reasons:

1   **We idolized them as the perfect person.**
2   **We expected them to change our lives and make us happy.**

This is asking too much from anything or anyone outside of ourselves. Diets are no different. When we read about a new "breakthrough" diet on Facebook or hear about it from a friend it's easy to hope that maybe this time we can succeed and reach our goal of a beautiful body that we're proud of, that makes us feel good about ourselves, that will free us to live the life we want (or so we believe). All our hopes are reinforced by the media and the so-called evidence of success around us. So the thought starts creeping up on us, "It's working for all these people, so it must be true – why not me?"

Thus the cycle begins again.

Maria's Story

When I met Maria, I saw the beautiful woman that she was, inside and out. But she was miserable. She was completely focused on losing weight and she had tried everything without results. She blamed herself and felt like a failure.

We started with the first step of self-acceptance and I shared some tools with her – *affirmations, mirror talk*, and the *5-second rule* (which we'll explore later in detail.) With her focus off the weight, she began to feel better. Her attitude and relationships improved, she regained an interest in the neglected aspects of her life. Within a few months, she had lost 20 pounds. The important thing to know is that the weight loss did NOT come from a diet but from her decision to love and trust herself and her body. Her inner goddess has awakened. She let go of the old story that she was a failure which allowed her to reclaim her confidence and, most importantly, to reconnect with a vision for her life. She followed her dream and went back to school to finish her education, an important goal that she had set aside.

Healing the Split

The obsessive cycle of dieting tends to create a split within us. On the one hand, you may have a strong belief about a certain diet or protocol—that it's somehow the key to your goal and yet at the same time you emotionally resist it. When you stubbornly hold to the belief, you try to convince yourself that it is the "right" thing in spite of the feeling you have. That's when the split happens because you are pulled in two opposite directions. Inner conflicts like this can happen in any area of our lives, be it a relationship, job, or other situation, causing us to get stuck. No movement can happen when we are pulled in opposite directions.

I remember the terrible feeling of resistance it caused in me when I felt compelled to adhere to a rigid and very restrictive diet that I believed was "correct" and, at the same time, I felt equally drawn to abandoning it because it was causing me so much pain.

Breaking the Cycle

If you are stuck in a cycle that you want to break, I hear you and I feel you, and I am here to tell you that you can end that cycle. If you are ready to go beyond temporary short-term results to achieve long-term well being, with a body you love and life you enjoy, I applaud you and I'm here to welcome you into the life you deserve. If you still believe there's a perfect diet or way of eating out there for you, you may need to continue your research. I wish you luck. But if you're ready to honor your uniqueness and reclaim your inherent power to create the life you want as an awakened goddess, let's get started.

The problem

IS NOT THE DIET ITSELF,

IT IS IT'S

Sustainability

Chapter Two

FOOD IS NOT THE ENEMY
Nature's Way is Pleasure

You have to suffer to be beautiful. Go on a green juice fast, stay away from grains, don't eat gluten or starchy vegetables, count calories, be hungry all the time, feel deprived, change the way you look, and exercise until you drop.

Sound familiar? Maybe those aren't the exact words but the messages we receive as women are pretty clear: Being beautiful, feeling good, and having the body you want is going to involve a lot of hard work and probably pain. It can't be avoided.

This belief has poisoned our relationship with the very substance created by our abundant earth to nourish us and keep us alive: Food. I am not talking about highly processed and packaged food full of artificial ingredients—I am talking about real food that is created by Mother Nature. Golden fields of wheat waving in the breeze are now feared because, over the last ten years, wheat has become the root of all evil. Potatoes, tomatoes and eggplants, essential ingredients in a lot of Middle Eastern cuisine, are now causing autoimmune disease and inflammation because they are "nightshades." Rice, the staple of Asian culture, is now deemed as the worst food to eat, beans contribute to "leaky gut" along with butternut squash, green peas, sweet potatoes which will make you fact because they are too "starchy." And the list goes on, as we create a problem for every food!

We have created food categories and attached scary labels which are now engraved in our mind! Labels for fat, labels for ugly, for disease, for inflammation. Food has become something we must control and punish ourselves with, something we fear. Definitely not something we could enjoy and treasure. Without realizing it, we have made food our enemy.

Most of us relate to this experience—I certainly do. I went through a period of years where I suffered and believed my suffering was necessary.

WE HAVE CREATED

Food Categories

AND ATTACHED SCARY LABELS WHICH ARE NOW
ENGRAVED IN OUR MIND! LABELS FOR FAT, LABELS
FOR UGLY, FOR DISEASE, FOR INFLAMMATION.
FOOD HAS BECOME SOMETHING WE MUST

Control and Punish

OURSELVES WITH, SOMETHING WE FEAR.
DEFINITELY NOT SOMETHING WE COULD

Enjoy and Treasure.

WITHOUT REALIZING IT, WE HAVE
MADE FOOD OUR

Enemy.

My Story

I grew up in Lebanon, a culture where it is very normal to make comments about somebody else's body. "Oh, you've gained weight! Better start a diet!" Or, "You are so skinny, you are going to break!" We even do this to little kids and teenagers. We do it with "good intentions" though, because of the strong cultural belief that a girl should be pretty first and foremost, or at minimum have a nice body.

When I was little, people told me I was ugly, sometimes openly, other times indirectly. So "ugly" in my own estimation, is what I became. I went from being super skinny in my pre-teen years to having "big thighs that hang" when I was a teenager. Comments like this hurt but then one day, in high school, I decided to love who I was, an act of rebellion against my family, my friends and everyone who thought I was not good enough. That little girl needed to survive.

I started focusing on the things I loved about myself, and that didn't only inspire me to be more creative in the way I expressed myself physically, but it also allowed my inner beauty to shine. By college, I have completely transformed, including my body language. Yes, I was able to change my physical appearance with my thoughts and a decision to love myself the way I am. Of course, the path in life is never a linear one. I shut down that fierce girl again toward the end of college when I went through some heartbreaks and experienced disappointments, my inner goddess sinking back in the belief that I was not good enough and that I need to be prettier, more successful, wealthier, funnier, thinner than I am.

I began to gain weight and the comments started.

> "You better be careful, you are becoming the size of a cow.
> "Your hips are getting so big."
> "Summer is coming you should start a diet and go to the gym."
> And so on.

My friends were all on diets but I loved food too much and could never stay on one for more than a few days. But the war inside of me was always alive, I felt guilty and like a constant failure because I couldn't diet successfully. I couldn't deprive myself so I started smoking a lot, using laxative teas and anything that would get rid of the food I was eating. I felt fat all the time with a constant feeling of shame and anxiety because I wasn't a size zero. Looking back at my pictures, I realize now that I never needed to lose weight. What had started out as a thought, became a belief, and then an obsession but had nothing to do with "reality."

Fast forward, in 2010, when I moved to the U.S. newly-married—my silent obsession about food got seriously triggered. No longer eating the home-cooked meals that my mom made from scratch, we were eating out in restaurants all the time: the flavors were overly processed, the portions huge, and I became fearful that I would start gaining weight again.

And because I have survived war, poverty, abuse and other traumas in my childhood, I underestimated the huge impact of the culture shock (not to mention marriage and moving to the other side of the world) I was experiencing. Here I was, married to the love of my life and living the so-called American dream. I should be in bliss, right? Soon after, I developed a severe rash on my neck that was irritating (and embarrassing, as I was a new bride!). I went to doctors, took medication, but the rash was stubborn and my anxiety was getting worse. A friend of mine suggested I cut out refined sugar, dairy, and meat. Even though I couldn't see how this could help me, I did it.

To my surprise, 10 days later, the rash faded. Then I grew curious and started doing some research and learned how food affects our health—this was especially important to me because soon I was pregnant with my first baby. Naturally, with the anxiety of a first mom, I wanted to do everything right. The first diet I landed on was the macrobiotic diet, and now I can see why I liked it so much: it promised perfect health so I followed it by the book, and yes, I lost a lot of weight, even though I was pregnant. In fact, throughout the whole pregnancy, I only gained 10 pounds and my baby was healthy. However, I didn't want to admit I was tired, looked pale most of the time, and hated the food I was eating. My diet was so restrictive and bland—brown rice with almost no salt, barley cooked in miso and carrots, oatmeal with no sweetener, no raw vegetables, no raw fruits, even the amount of water was restricted. There was also a rule that you had to chew each bite 100 times, which felt like pure punishment instead of nourishment.

Not only that, this diet, like most other diets, tries to make you believe it is the one and only, and if you stop or change it, you will gain back all the weight or get sick.

It's like an abusive partner that convinces you that leaving them will ruin your life. So you stay even though you are suffering because you believe them and you are scared.

At that time in my life, I wasn't connected to my inner goddess at all. I felt powerless, unworthy, and not deserving of the good things in life. All I wanted was to feel safe in this big country where nothing was familiar, isn't it interesting how we are wired to turn to food to comfort us, to make us feel secure? **But it is not what we "want" that manifests, as I was to learn later, it is what we "believe".**

Towards the end of my pregnancy, I was completely exhausted but I didn't want to admit it. My body felt weak, I struggled with breastfeeding and didn't have enough energy to take care of a newborn but I pushed myself (because that's what we women usually do) and this took a toll on my body. Then I got really confused: how could this happen since I'm following a diet that claims wellness and vitality! I convinced myself that nothing was wrong with the diet but *with me*, and as a result, I became even more strict as a way to *punish* myself.

Two years later, literally fed up, I turned to a vegan diet, which was more attractive, especially for my *Instagram feed:* more colors and flavor combinations were allowed. Finally out from under the rigid rules of a macrobiotic diet, I was soon binging on formerly forbidden fruits: sometimes 10 bananas a day, gulping smoothies by the tons, going on a watermelon island (eating only watermelon for days), water fast for 3 days, eating only raw food for a year. I tried every cleansing method I could find because I believed that I had to keep detoxing, stay in control, and deprive myself so I wouldn't get sick or fat. It became a serious addiction. My weight under control, I became very popular on Instagram and took my cooking skills to another level, studying raw food cuisine and making my own raw vegan aged cheese and raw chocolate at home.

As my interest in nutrition grew, I enrolled in the *Institute for Integrative Nutrition* and studied over 100 dietary theories. A sea of questions arose.

Why were these different experts so convinced and passionate about their particular nutrition theory?

Which one was right?—they couldn't all be.

Why do some people thrive on a diet while others don't?

Why do some people, following a "healthy" diet by the book, still suffer from various diseases?

Why people, on a certain protocol, lose all the weight, only to gain it back a year later?

Meanwhile, I have moved to the East Coast from sunny California, my husband was away for work, I was taking care of two babies and was facing some challenges in life while working on myself. I got diagnosed with adrenal fatigue, and a nutritionist friend suggested I switch to the Paleo diet as a possible remedy. Though I had a distaste and repugnance for meat since childhood, I gave it a try because I was desperate. It also gave me hope since many "experts" praised the Paleo diet. I was suffering, not knowing what to eat for breakfast anymore (eggs were forbidden). Needless to say, I couldn't stay long on that diet, not only because I hated what I was eating but also because I started gaining weight like never before in my life.

After a while, I came to understand I was giving food way more than it could handle: I had put it on a pedestal thinking that all my problems started and ended there! Finally, I came to the following realizations or in better words, these realizations were just in my face and I couldn't ignore them anymore:

> *Our body and whole being feed on more than the food on our plate, no matter how healthy or "good" it is.*
>
> *Food is not the hero or the enemy.*
>
> *Food should remain pleasurable or else it will turn into poison.*
>
> *Obsessing over what we put in our mouth is not healthy.*
>
> *Our body shouldn't be controlled, it should be loved.*

It took me a while to come to these epiphanies, years to realize that there is much more to our well-being than the food that we eat. And while the food we choose to give ourselves is still important, it is only a small percentage of the equation. We can give the healthiest food to our body, but if we are constantly hating it, thinking negative thoughts and operating from a place of fear, food won't take us far in our endeavor. A hated body will never feel well or nourished no matter how "healthy" you feed it.

HAS FOOD BECOME YOUR ENEMY?

People have different results with dieting. Maybe you've tried a diet, followed it by the book, a diet that all your friends had great results with, but it didn't work for you. Perhaps without realizing, like me, you've made food your enemy.

To find out, ask yourself these questions:

Are you following the diet rigidly and bashing yourself if you don't see results?

Are you putting pressure on yourself every time you get on that scale and see no difference?

Do you feel that that diet is actually depriving you and leaving you unnourished and unsatisfied?

Are you afraid that something is wrong with you?

Do you fear that a certain food will cause disease or make you gain weight?

Are you constantly thinking about food and feeling confused about what to eat?

Do you feel like it's an unpleasant chore every time you have to deal with meal preparation: what ingredients to buy, what to cook, how to cook it? Do you alternate between deprivation and binging?

Do you believe that you will never look and feel amazing despite all the "healthy" food you are eating?

Do you feel like no matter what diet you are on, nothing seems to work for you?

If you answer yes to *any* of these questions, you have made food your enemy. The reason you fail to get results is because you are divided within yourself and your body will not cooperate in that state. So the first thing you have to do is to create a new relationship with what you put in our mouth. To stop being in a constant state of obsession or terror every time we have to deal with food, which is three times a day.

Do you remember how you experienced your meals when you were a child? You ate with pure pleasure and excitement, trusting that your parents or caregivers were giving you food that was good for you, and after you were finished, you didn't think about food anymore, except for saying how good it was. I promise you can feel this way again. In the same way that you trusted your caregivers, you can rebuild that trust directly in Mother Nature. The truth you've forgotten is that food is not something to fear, it is not something to obsess over, it is not something to attach our emotions to, expectations and fears on. Food is supposed to fuel and nourish our body, and yes, give us pleasure.

So why do we need to detox?

IT IS NOT "WHAT" WE

Want

THAT MANIFESTS,

IT IS WHAT WE

Believe.

Chapter Three

THE TRUTH ABOUT DETOXIFICATION
Letting Go What No Longer Serves You

What comes to mind when you hear the word detoxification? Maybe you think about the quality of food or water—are they healthy or toxic? The dictionary offers this view: "Abstaining from drink and drugs until the bloodstream is free of toxins, in order to overcome addictions or become free of harmful substances." If your aim is to lose weight and create a healthier body, your thoughts probably go to the foods you need to eliminate from your diet in order to "cleanse" or "heal" your body. During the years I was caught up in rigid dieting and detoxifying, I shared a similar and limiting perspective.

My current new (and very liberating) view is that *detoxification* is a process that includes our whole being: it can't be reduced to a drink, a particular food, a potion or a magic pill! Simply put, it is letting go of anything that adds resistance to your natural ability to thrive—body, mind, and soul. Because, yes, you came here to thrive through it all.

What I discovered—and why I've written this book—is a different way, a transformational way of looking at detoxification. This is not to deny the truth that when we consistently put foods that create toxins in our body, toxins beyond which our body can process, we will experience a host of unpleasant symptoms, from brain fog to weight gain. But there is another element that is overlooked about the food we feed our minds with: *our thoughts*. Toxic thoughts are as harmful, and perhaps more harmful to us than what we put into our mouths. What, does that sound extreme?

DETOXIFICATION IS

Letting Go

OF ANYTHING THAT ADDS RESISTANCE

TO YOUR NATURAL ABILITY TO

THRIVE—BODY, MIND, AND SOUL.

BECAUSE, YES, YOU CAME HERE TO

Thrive Through It All.

One of my biggest discoveries about detoxing came to me when I realized that it wasn't a certain food or substance I needed to detox from but rather the rigid dogmas and labels about food that were keeping me from evolving. And while I still eat 90% a plant-based diet, I do it because it is just the way I enjoy eating, not because I have to, not because I feel compelled to follow a certain set of rules.

Health is about your entire lifestyle: how you feel, what you believe, the words you say, the energy you emanate, your ability to dream and follow your dream. To detox is to let go of what no longer serves you so you can be in alignment with the body and life you want to create.

HEALTH IS ABOUT YOUR

Entire LifeStyle

HOW YOU FEEL, WHAT YOU BELIEVE,
THE WORDS YOU SAY, THE ENERGY
YOU EMANATE, YOUR ABILITY TO
DREAM AND FOLLOW YOUR DREAM.

To Detox

IS TO LET GO OF WHAT NO LONGER
SERVES YOU SO YOU CAN BE IN
ALIGNMENT WITH THE BODY AND
LIFE YOU WANT

To Create.

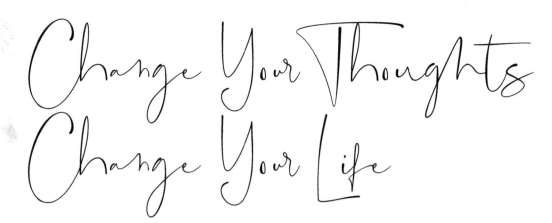

Change Your Thoughts Change Your Life

When I came upon the work of Abraham Hicks (law of attraction), I began to develop spiritual awareness. Before I opened up to the idea that I was more than just a physical body, I didn't realize the effects of the disabling fear of what would happen if I ate the "wrong, unhealthy" food. With my punishing thoughts, I was poisoning myself far worse than any food could. I learned about the power of self-love from Louise Hay and started using positive affirmations and keeping a gratitude journal. My world expanded exponentially, as I began to nourish my spirit.

Affirmations are an amazing practice that helped me shift my perspective from fear to love and from toxicity to healing. Through daily use, I started to tap into my own power to create the health and life I wanted, no longer at the mercy of diets or the tyranny of dogma because no matter what happened I was building the confidence and faith in my own ability to transform it.

A few of the powerful affirmations that altered my attitude slowed me down and allowed me to begin to hear my own inner wisdom speaking to me:

"My body is so smart at doing its job. I fully trust my body."

"Life is always working out for me in the best way possible."

"I appreciate and love all the seasons and cycles my body go through"

"I love how my body is an indicator of my own vibration, on happy days it is thriving and vibrant, on out of alignment days it is not compliant and out of tune"

"I appreciate how my body is calling me back to practice unconditional love"

"I am always being taken care of."

"I am experiencing vibrant health every day."

As these statements created new thoughts and insights, a big burden lifted from my shoulders and heart. I stopped expecting myself to be perfect, stopped trying to figure out and control everything, which is of course not only impossible but also exhausting! Better choices came effortlessly and I stopped freaking out when I made a "mistake" because I also learned that mistakes are just fine-tuning to catch the right frequency.

It wasn't until I started feeding my soul in this way, and not only my body, that things started shifting. Not that I stopped going through the ups and downs of life, no, but I learned from the downs to manifest more of what I wanted and to realign with my higher self. My fears no longer imprisoned me.

I no longer believed that food alone determined my health, or how my body looked: we are much more powerful than that.

You may think this new freedom steered me away from eating healthy, but the opposite happened.

I NO LONGER BELIEVED THAT

Food Alone

DETERMINED MY HEALTH, OR HOW MY

BODY LOOKED: WE ARE MUCH MORE

Powerful

THAN THAT.

Your Birthright: Abundance and Vitality

As my spiritual awareness developed, my thoughts and beliefs altered. I connected with the power and beauty of my body. I was no longer a victim; I owned my choices, past and present. I am not ashamed of them, I love them and honor them as part of my path, and when the "not so pleasant" ones arise, I recognize them as the most important factors in my evolution. I came to understand and witness that my thoughts and beliefs created (and create) every single event in my life.

I started to manifest flow and abundance in my life. No, I didn't marry a rich guy (even though that could be a way to manifest abundance and there's nothing wrong with it), my husband was unemployed when I first married him. Sharing with others my experience and discoveries, my coaching business thrived. As I tapped more into the abundance mindset, my husband joined me and we started manifesting more and more of it. Today, we both have thriving careers and we are at a place we could not have imagined nine years ago. Now our choices come from a place of inspiration and self-love, not a place of restriction or limitation.

Awaken Your Inner Goddess

Here are the insights that changed my life and can change yours and awaken your Inner Goddess:

Food is just one piece of the puzzle.
It's not all the puzzle.

Self-love and self-acceptance are
inherent to a happy healthy life.

We can change our reality by changing
our thoughts and not the
other way around.

We are worthy just the way we are.

Our actions should be inspired and not
forced in order to get results
for the long term.

Gratitude will help us navigate from
where we are to where we want to be
because no change is instant.

Manifesting the body and health we
want starts in our mind.

This doesn't mean we no longer experience feelings of guilt, shame, disappointments, anger, sadness or fear, but these emotions no longer have a huge negative impact on us. We learn to calm and tame them.

"It's ok," you say to your disappointment, "Next time, we will choose better."

"Don't worry," you can say to your guilt, "It's part of our learning experience."

"There is nothing to be ashamed of," you will say to shame, "We are all in this together."

"Ok," I see you are angry, "What change needs to occur here?"

"I am here for you," you will say to fear, "We are going to be alright, as we have always been."

"It's not really hatred that we are feeling, it is just a call to love more," we will say to hatred.

Everyday day we wake up (and go to sleep) in the environment of our thoughts. Once we understand their profound effects and our ability to change them, we experience freedom. In the next chapter, we will look more deeply at this phenomenon.

Chapter Four

THE POWER OF THE MIND
Freedom from Negative Self Talk

In 2019, I attended Tony Robbins' *Unleash the Power Within* four-day event, 8 am to midnight. The first day was very special as it ends with the famous fire-walk. I came that day doubting that I would really do it because come on, why would I ever risk getting my feet burned by red-hot 1000-degree coals? But I still put my slippers on because I had the desire to overcome my fear. Whether or not I would overcome it was another question.

At midnight on Day One, after spending hours getting pumped and motivated along with 15,000 other people, the time came. Tony warned us that if we didn't believe we wouldn't get burned, the odds were that we would. I didn't want to hear that! What if my mind didn't fully believe I could do it? The fear of pain was terrifying.

I was there with a friend and I decided to go home which was a 45-minute drive, take a shower, and get some sleep so I'd be ready for Day 2. We took off toward the room where our belongings were but the way was blocked. Instead, we were told to go around which meant we had to walk past the firewalk lanes.

I felt so frustrated and angry, I just wanted to get out of there!

Suddenly and unexpectedly, I found myself standing in a line, and in a second my thoughts shifted from: "What if I get burned?" to "What if I can?" to "I can do it!" I began repeating "Yes, Yes, Yes!" along with the thousands of people around me. When it was my turn, I totally committed and walked with a determined focus across the coals repeating "cool moss," as Tony had taught us, and it was over.

I didn't get burned.

Was I 100% not afraid? No.
Was I 100% ready? No.
Was I 100% sure that my feet wouldn't burn? No.

How Did I Do It?

There was actually a lot of preparation, as I reflected later on the experience. We were led through a powerful visualization where we imagined the whole process in detail. I saw myself walking on the coals and being totally fine, no fear, no burning. To create confidence, we were told to walk with our heads up, not down. He also had us name the hot red coals, "cool moss," and keep repeating it over and over, along with, "Yes, yes, yes!" This is effective because when you change the words you give to a situation, a feeling, a thought or a thing, it changes your perception of it, affects the way you feel about it, and your physiology actually changes.

Perhaps you've had the experience when you were in school of noticing a student constantly being criticized by the teacher. The result? The student performs poorly and misbehaves. The next year, the same student with low grades and difficult behavior shines because their new teacher, seeing their gifts and potential, encourages them and believes in them. Suddenly the student seems like a different person!

> *In the same way, if you call yourself ugly or a failure, and you believe it, that's what you will eventually manifest in your life.*

Your body and your whole being are always listening and processing the information you are providing, absorbing your words and the attitude behind them. Like many of us growing up, you may have heard negative words repeated over and over—unkind (and untrue) criticisms such as, "You're not smart," or "You aren't pretty enough." Eventually, we come to believe these statements and say them to ourselves, usually without realizing it. But now you can choose the ones you want to believe in!

There's a simple test. Let every word, every thought pass through a new filter that asks: does it come from love or hate? If it comes from love and appreciation, let it through, if it comes from judgment and fear let it go.

IF YOU CALL YOURSELF UGLY

OR A FAILURE, AND YOU

Believe It

THAT'S WHAT YOU WILL EVENTUALLY

Manifest in Your Life.

The Rice Experiment

Here's another proof point which convinced me of the power of our words, thoughts, and intentions. Several years ago, Dr. Masaru Emoto, a popular researcher and author, demonstrated the literal power of thought in his rice experiments, which have been reproduced by many people since then with different variations. I was curious but approached it with skepticism. It's quite simple.

I cooked some rice, let it cool and filled two identical jars with an equal amount. On the first jar, I wrote: *Thank you, I love you.* On the second jar, I wrote: *I hate you, you fool!* I closed the jars and placed them side by side on my kitchen counter. Every day, I sent the message of love to the first jar and the message of hate to the second one. I would look at each one and say the message out loud with the corresponding energy and intention.

The first three days nothing happened, and I started to think how foolish I was for even trying such a ridiculous experiment. But on the fifth day, to my surprise, I opened the two jars and I was in shock! The first jar, to which I was constantly sending love vibes, had barely some pink mold while the second jar, to which I was constantly sending hate vibes, had prominent black mold.

It became clear to me that our cells thrive or become dis-eased according to what we are saying and thinking. "I hate you" will darken our cells, make them struggle and shrink while "I love and accept you" bathes them in crystal light and well-being.

This experiment completely changed not only the way I look at the words I use but my intentions as well. I encourage you not to take my word for it, however, and to try it yourself! Get your kids, your partner, and your parents on board to make it a fun and bonding activity.

IT BECAME

Clear to Me

THAT OUR CELLS THRIVE OR BECOME

DI-SEASED ACCORDING TO WHAT WE ARE

Saying and Thinking

"I HATE YOU" WILL DARKEN OUR CELLS, MAKE THEM

STRUGGLE AND SHRINK WHILE

"I LOVE AND ACCEPT YOU" BATHES THEM IN

Crystal Light

AND WELL-BEING.

Wake Up!

What these two experiences revealed to me is the fact that whatever change I was seeking had to come from inside me. There was no magic diet, exercise workout, success program, or job that was going to create the peace and fulfillment that I wanted—except for awakening to my powerful and beautiful inner goddess; she is the ultimate creator.

So the burning question becomes:

Where does your focus go? What power are you giving to the things you don't want? What power are you giving to the things you want to create in your life? What negative self-talk is running your life (into the ground), leading you where you don't want to go?

When I realized the devastating effects of my negative self-talk, it became an urgent matter for me to consciously form the thoughts I knew would create the life I wanted. I was no longer a victim of what other people told me I needed. What a freedom! I began to reclaim my power, my connection to my intuition, and to rejoice in my ability to listen to my body. I stopped looking for truth outside of myself—it's that simple and yet utterly profound.

I have always believed that Mother Nature has all the answers we are looking for. Have you ever seen an animal in the wild going to a dietitian or looking for the latest diet trend? Of course not. Why? Because all living beings are part of nature and nature doesn't need a manual or instructions in order to live and thrive, it just does!

And this is who we are, we are part of nature, aren't we? We have the same wisdom and well-being in our genes and soul, we just need to remember our power and connect with our inner goddess.

The reason why many of us fail at manifesting the weight, health, relationship, money or career we want is that, along the way, we forgot who we are, we gave up our power, we accepted the answers that were given to us and thus became more confused than ever. We fell prey to the conditioning that we are small, incapable and victims of our fate. No longer.

In the exercise below, I invite you to take a look at the thoughts and beliefs that are preventing you from having or achieving what you want. For example, if you want to be wealthy, it might be that you think wealthy people are greedy or selfish or that you believe you don't deserve wealth. In this case, even though you want to become rich, the vibration you are offering is contradictory to the desire itself and so without realizing you are fighting your own desire.

Which is why sometimes, an immediate change of thought may not work because your vibration has already gained momentum and continues to do so.

What is one thing you strongly desire but think you can never do or have?
Write it down.

Do you get scared, anxious or discouraged at the thought of it?

Then give 3 reasons you believe you cannot have it or become it.
Write your answers down.

One

Two

Three

On a scale from 1 to 10, how much do you think those beliefs are serving your desire? Are they empowering or disempowering? Zero being not serving them at all and 10 being absolutely serving them.

0   1   2   3   4   5   6   7   8   9   10

What are the feelings that arise when you listed the above answers?
Feelings: (up to 5)

One

Two

Three

Four

Five

Write down how you could change those beliefs to support your desires
(even if you don't really believe in them right now).

One

Two

Three

On a scale from 1 to 10, how much do you think those thoughts are serving
your desire? Are they empowering or disempowering? 0 being not serving
them at all and 10 being absolutely serving them.

0   1   2   3   4   5   6   7   8   9   10

Read them out loud.

Now, spend a few moments thinking about what you could you do or say to "prime" yourself so you can see yourself achieving, having or being the thing that you desire?

In other words, what are the necessary preparations that you need to do to ease your mind and help it believe otherwise?

Write them down.

One

Two

Three

NOTE: If you get stuck, reverse the situation and imagine a friend has come to you asking your help with this problem or goal. What would you say to them? How would you encourage them?

Feel free to express yourself by drawing below.

Chapter Five

WORKING WITH ENERGY
Why Vibration Is the Real Change

> My grandma used to say, "If you are upset, do not cook, because the food is going to taste like your anger."

This ancient, cultural wisdom brilliantly defines the underlying principle of what today is spoken of as "energy" or "vibration."

In the same way, the "vibration" of our environment exerts a powerful effect on us. But the good news is that we get to pick and choose which vibration we want to focus upon. You probably know the saying: *where focus goes, energy flows*.

High vibrations are generally associated with positive qualities and feelings, such as love, peace, appreciation, abundance, ease and joy. Low vibrations are associated with darker emotions such as anger, fear, hatred, judgment, lack and despair. The higher your vibration, the more in alignment (or harmony) you are with your inner Being or what is usually described as *living in the flow*. The lower your vibration, the more out of sync you are with your highest self, and therefore the more conflict, struggle and overall "stuckness" you will experience in life.

Real Food Has Energy

Food is a major life experience that affects our well being. Food from nature has a higher vibration whereas packaged or processed food has a lower vibration. Let me give you an example: have you ever tried to grow food from vegetable scraps? If not, I would like you to try it!

> *The next time you chop lettuce for a salad, scallions, carrots, celery, or onions, select a scrap and place it in water. A couple of days later you will notice that it starts growing into the vegetable again! Try it with cheerios.*

Real (living) food nurtures you; "fake" (nonliving) food does not. That's pretty easy to understand and accept. However, another aspect of vibration which emanates from our feelings, intentions and thoughts is more elusive—and yet more significant than the food itself.

My mom was a teacher. As a busy working mom, she had five to six meals on her menu that she cooked over and over, most of them stews with rice. I always wondered why the same meal she made would sometimes taste delicious and at other times be tasteless. Now I understand that her overall energy, how she was feeling, affected the food she was making even though she was making it *exactly the same way.* On days when she was tired, the food was bland; on happy days, it tasted great.

You may notice something similar.

> *A food that you usually avoid because it causes you some discomfort, when enjoyed with friends or family on a very happy day, may not affect you at all.*

Has this ever happened to you?

I had a recent conversation with a friend for whom nightshades like eggplant and tomatoes are a big NO. I asked her if there was a time when she ate tomatoes and they didn't bother her. Her first answer was: No! I invited her to think about it again and she said: Well, yes, sometimes, especially when I don't know it is there! This is the placebo effect we are all familiar with. When we expect a certain reaction from a food or medicine, we are likely to experience it. My friend, not knowing the tomatoes were in the food, had no reason to expect a negative reaction, so it didn't happen: mind over matter.

This principle demonstrates that the food you choose to eat is not as important as the energy you create around it.

> *Even if I'm eating the healthiest food I can find, but I'm feeling deprived and fearful, that food is not going to fully nourish me.*

Consider that even grains of rice respond to what we think or say, to our intentions of encouragement or disgust. Or that through the power of belief, a person can walk over coals and not get burned. I certainly would not have believed if I had not experienced it.

How Vibration Is Created

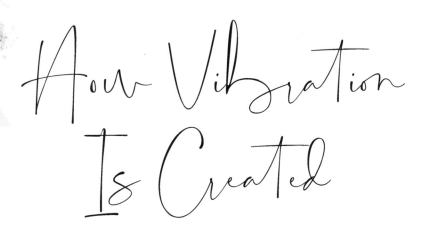

While a living food, such as broccoli or beets, has a high vibration in itself, the way we experience that food is determined by the way we interact with it: the way we grow it, handle it, prepare it and, as importantly, the way we think about it, eat it, process it and assimilate it.

Person A is eating a kale salad and some of the repetitive thoughts and emotions that rule her life in general and the eating situation in particular are:

I hate my body, I look horrible.

I hate eating this food but I am going to eat it because it is supposed to make me lose the weight.

*I love bread but **gluten is bad**, it is going to destroy my gut health. I know I shouldn't be eating it, but I am going to eat it anyway. I've already probably gained weight.*

I ate too many calories today, I am definitely gaining weight.

I am so exhausted from thinking about the food I am eating or I am going to eat.

I hate eating.

Person B is eating a kale salad, a delicious spaghetti pomodoro, and enjoying a piece of bread with some olive oil. Some of the thoughts and emotions that rule her life in general and the eating situation in particular are:

I love this food. It is so delicious. What a pleasure it is to eat and nourish my body with fuel and vitality.

My body knows how to metabolize this food perfectly.

I no longer feel hungry, my body feels satisfied.

I am so thankful for the abundance of choices I have.

I love food and food loves me.

I love my body and I am grateful for all the things it does for me.

My body is the physical expression of me. I love how unique and beautiful I look.

While both of these people have the same desire to be healthy, feel good, and look good in their body, it's obvious that the vibration Person A creates with her thoughts and emotions completely contradicts her desire whereas Person B is emitting a vibration that is a match to her desire.

Person A's thoughts and emotions are vibrating: hate, guilt, fear, remorse, and disempowerment.

Person B's thoughts and emotions are vibrating: love, appreciation, gratitude, trust, empowerment, and satisfaction.

Regardless of the evidence around us, it's easy to see ourselves as victims of our circumstances: how our partner behaves, the kind of job we have (or don't have), the way our body looks or how we feel when we get up in the morning. We find it difficult to believe that we can create our reality and achieve our dreams.

But the basic principle of life is this: Every (and any) change you want to make in your life, whatever you desire and want to achieve, starts from the inside and comes **directly from the choices you make and how you are lining up with those choices** (which is your vibration). The words you use, the thoughts you think, the feelings you choose to feel and the intentions you bring to your situation create your experience, be it a fleeting mood, the complex chemistry of your body or the meal you are making. This incredible freedom has been given to us and it's our choice how we will use it.

Once you accept this, you become the artist of your life.

Reclaim Your Power

Whatever it is you desire starts with energy and vibration. The degree of manifestation depends on the agreement between the vibration you are emanating and the the actions you take.

The stronger the match between them, the more powerful the result. So if your goal is to create a beautiful body and experience vibrant, glowing health and well-being, *you have to warm up your vibration* for that reality to ensure that you are totally lined up with your goal. The general guideline in all cases is to make peace with the food on your plate or in your shopping bag: line up with it, focus and affirm the good aspects of it or else don't eat it.

Because if you are going to eat it anyway, dwelling on your fear of how it will affect you will eliminate any potentially positive aspects it may have. It doesn't matter if it's ice cream or kale!

Owning our choices, past and present, is a first step towards freedom, change and awakening.

OWNING OUR CHOICES

Past and Present

IS A FIRST STEP TOWARDS FREEDOM,

CHANGE AND

Awakening.

Chapter Six

AWAKENING THE GODDESS
Are You Ready for Empowerment?

Who is the goddess?

She isn't a stranger or an ideal you can never become. She isn't someone on a pedestal who evokes your envy or who makes you feel disempowered.

The goddess is the unedited expression of your true self before the world (parents, religion, society, peers, education) told you who you were or who you should be.

Do you remember yourself at a young age when you were free, joyous, present in the moment, shining with joie de vivre and unconditional love towards yourself and everyone around you?

Close your eyes, see that girl, how old is she? What is she wearing? What's the expression on her face? What is she doing? How is she feeling?

Now, remember a moment in your life when that goddess got shut down, where she started feeling scared, hurt, abandoned, small, ashamed, unworthy, hating and doubting herself. (Tears may happen, release them without judgment).

Now give this shut-down girl a name, (your name), let's say D. Years forward, D took over, in her need to protect herself, to fit in, to prove she was worthy, to compete until she was exhausted, in search of appreciation and acceptance, trying SO HARD to be everything others want her to be and maybe nothing like she is.

The Goddess

IS THE UNEDITED EXPRESSION OF
YOUR TRUE SELF BEFORE THE WORLD
(PARENTS, RELIGION, SOCIETY, PEERS,
EDUCATION) TOLD YOU WHO YOU
WERE OR WHO YOU

Should Be.

What happened?

She puts the Goddess within her to sleep. And the more judgment, disappointment, heartache, and sorrow got buried under the layers of ego armor, the more disconnected she became from her true self.

Can you see both of them? Which one feels more like home to you? The one who continually struggles to be or to do, always feeling that she'll never be enough no matter what-- or the one who feels powerful just the way she is?

If your answer is the latter, then I invite you to wake up Goddess (your name) now. She's been waiting for you, she is the real you, she is the real expression of who you are before you were trained to be what others believed you were supposed to be.

Let her take that hurt, scared little girl in her arms and give her a big, comforting hug, all the while telling her gently and with love, that you are there for her, will always be there for her, no matter what happens. You will not abandon her again, smother or mask her identity, push down her joie de vivre, forget or discard her worth. No. Instead, you will love her unconditionally and allow her to fully embrace her journey back to love.

You are now Awakened Goddess!

Are you ready to connect with her and pursue your dreams? That means you are willing to be YOUR BEST FRIEND, through the good and the bad, the ups and the downs. Making that commitment is essential because doubt and resistance will emerge to challenge you on your journey until you fully embody her again like you did before you shut her down.

Remember the story of Maria? She tried everything to lose weight but all her efforts failed—and she was miserable. Her inner goddess had not yet awakened. In our work together, she didn't focus on food or weight. She began with the decision to love her body and trust herself. Using the tools and practices of the goddess, she started loving parts of herself she had ignored under the "I hate my body" label. She got busy raising her vibration by choosing better thoughts and feeling good feelings. She tapped into self-acceptance and self-forgiveness by unlearning the many hurtful beliefs and damaging dogmas she had acquired in pursuit of what others said she should be, do, think, feel, believe, or look. She regained interest in the neglected aspects of her life and went back to school to finish her education, an important goal that she had set aside.

*Within a few months, she lost 20 pounds, but the thing to know is that the weight loss did NOT come from controlling what she ate or didn't eat, but from her decision to love and trust herself. Most importantly, she learned she could give herself a chance every time she thought she failed or messed up because **as a goddess**, as her own beloved, she knew she deserved unlimited chances on her journey to reach her goals and fulfills her desires.*

She came to understand that central to her success and happiness was inner harmony. Step by step, she learned to align every part of herself: thoughts, feelings, beliefs, and actions to consciously create a unified, high vibration, a vibration based on the principle of self-love. For it is love that aligns us with the universe and our deepest heart and spirit, allowing our talents and dreams to come forth.

Will you take that journey to awaken the goddess within you? She has been waiting for so long and the time has come now.

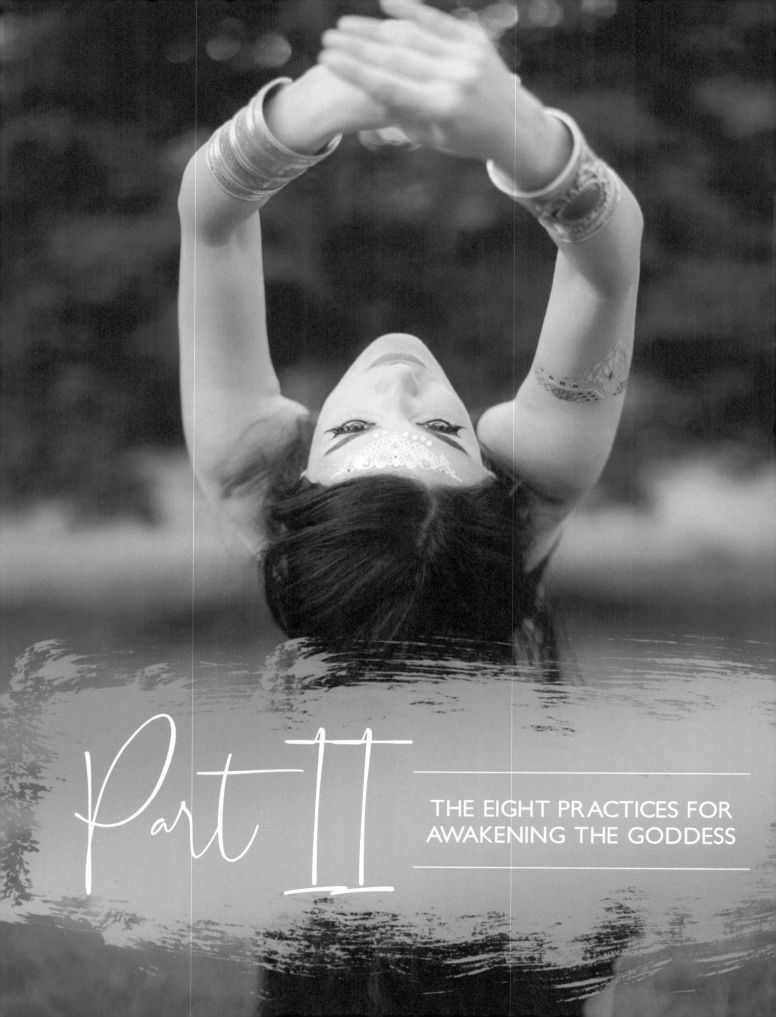

Part II

THE EIGHT PRACTICES FOR AWAKENING THE GODDESS

The Eight Practices

These eight exercises empower you in two essential ways: 1) they will help you to let go of your resistance to change and 2) they will awaken your inner goddess. Some of these practices, such as *mirror talk*, I learned and adapted from the great Louise Hay and from which I was inspired to create another technique that I call "mirror dance therapy" which cultivates body love and acceptance. Others, such as Food Rituals, I developed for myself and my clients. I invite you to give each a try and by doing so, claim your power and raise your vibration. Thus you'll be on your way to fully awakening your Goddess Self!

These exercises also serve as the ideal preparation for The Detoxification Protocol of Part III since there is no more important element to detoxify from than dogmas and false beliefs about food and our body, self-hatred, negative self-dialogue, and blame.

1. Affirmations

2. Mirror Talk

3. Mirror Dance

4. Food Rituals

5. The 5-Second Rule

6. Body Movement

7. Visualizations

8. Appreciation Journal

It Will Take Time

We are all eager for change, to realize our full potential for joy and ease as soon as possible. I support you in moving toward that goal with enthusiasm and confidence—and also with the acceptance and understanding that it takes time. The long term benefit is that when we allow ourselves the time to cultivate change it will be more sustainable and fun.

The reasons why it will take time:

We have been disconnected for a long time from ourselves, relying on external resources.

We are uniquely created, therefore every body's needs are different.

We go through big changes, especially as women throughout the month and throughout our life.

Life is so busy and noisy, it takes commitment and self-love to connect to one's self.

AFFIRMATIONS

Before you can change your lifestyle and manifest your dreams — you have to believe it's possible, which for most of us means we have to change our negative self-talk and put something new (and truthful) in its place to redirect our thinking and feeling. Affirmations are a primary tool to do that.

To quote Louise Hay's definition:

"Put simply, whatever we say or think is an affirmation. All of your self-talk, the dialogue in your head, is a stream of affirmations."

Many of us don't realize that words have the power to change our vibration. We are all programmed and trained to think, feel, and behave in certain ways—some we are aware of and some we are not. Affirmations are deliberate messages to your subconscious that retrain your old programming. Repeated daily (or several times a day), affirmations release the internal and external blockages that prevent you from living your life as the goddess that you are. **When you allow negative self-talk, your goddess shuts down.**

For example:

I am so fat and I look horrible, nobody is ever going to like me with a body like this. I look so ugly, I am a failure, I am inferior to other women, my boyfriend is definitely going to cheat on me, I do not look sexy, I hate myself. It's hopeless, I'm hopeless.

If you have been saying things to yourself like the above, when you first start replacing these negative thoughts with more positive and hopeful ones, it's going to feel awkward and not authentic. It may even feel like you are lying to yourself. It's just your ego trying to protect you from what is not familiar. Acknowledge it, thank it and keep working with the positive affirmations anyway.

Affirmations

ARE DELIBERATE MESSAGES TO YOUR

SUBCONSCIOUS THAT RETRAIN YOUR

OLD PROGRAMMING.

If you have been saying things to yourself like the above, when you first start replacing these negative thoughts with more positive and hopeful ones, it's going to feel awkward and not authentic. It may even feel like you are lying to yourself. It's just your ego trying to protect you from what is not familiar. Acknowledge it, thank it and keep working with the positive affirmations anyway.

When we have been hating our body or ourselves for so long, it may be difficult to shift to a loving attitude right away so begin with the one thing that you love about yourself or your body and focus on it. Just be willing to practice, starting where you feel you can start and building from there.

For example:

I really love my eyes, their color, shape, or the way they sparkle. Then feel appreciation for that.

Let's say you don't like your bloated tummy, and you have been feeling all the negative feelings and talking all the depreciating talk about it and to it:

I hate how bloated I am, I look horrible in almost all my clothes because of the fat belly I have. I hate taking pictures because of my bloated tummy. If only I could get rid of this stupid belly, it makes me look so ugly, everybody will notice it and think I am a fat loser.

Now imagine what effect this talk has on you, your self-esteem, your cells, your belly itself?

While manifesting a "not bloated belly" will take time, you don't need to wait until then to start shifting your self-talk. I understand how hard it is to love something unless it is loveable according to what you have been taught is loveable. In this case, you could appreciate another aspect of that area other than its shape. For example,

> *My belly is so special because it had the amazing ability to expand and make room for my babies to grow.*
>
> *Or:*
>
> *I appreciate that my tummy and body have survived all the weird diets and practices (laxative herbs, diet pills, appetite suppressors and more) I have it put it through, especially the side effects they have had on my digestion and overall body image.*
>
> *I am grateful for such a resilient body that deserves love and compassion from me.*

After you have practiced this vibration a while, you will begin to feel the love and tap into the energy of the positive feeling. Then there will come a day when you can say: I FULLY LOVE AND ACCEPT MY BODY and mean it! It may even come sooner than you expect. Just keep an open heart and mind.

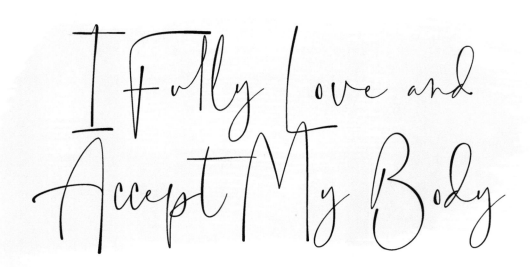

I Fully Love and Accept My Body

I AM GRATEFUL FOR SUCH A

Resilient Body

THAT DESERVES

Love and

Compassion

FROM ME.

AFFIRMATIONS

Write three affirmations that you will use every day for the next 30 days, getting inspiration from the examples mentioned above.

Or choose one of the 3 following affirmations:

I am a work in progress. I am constantly evolving and getting better every day.

My body is unique and it is the expression of how I feel on the inside. I choose to feel good and be appreciative of all that is.

I am excited about the work I am doing on myself. I love my ability to choose the things that I want more of in my life and focus on them.

If you realize that it is 3 pm and you forgot to do your affirmations at noon (your midday time), forgive yourself immediately and just do them.

One [ ]

Two [ ]

Three [ ]

Affirmations

I AM A WORK IN PROGRESS. I AM
CONSTANTLY EVOLVING AND
GETTING BETTER EVERY DAY.

MY BODY IS UNIQUE AND IT IS THE
EXPRESSION OF HOW I FEEL ON THE
INSIDE. I CHOOSE TO FEEL GOOD AND
BE APPRECIATIVE OF ALL THAT IS.

I AM EXCITED ABOUT THE WORK I AM
DOING ON MYSELF. I LOVE MY ABILITY
TO CHOOSE THE THINGS THAT I WANT
MORE OF IN MY LIFE AND FOCUS
ON THEM.

MIRROR TALK

Mirror talk is another way of using affirmations by looking directly in the mirror as you say them. This powerful method of self-love was first created and made popular by Louise Hay. She developed a 21-day practice of looking in the mirror for healing low self-esteem.

"Because the mirror reflects back to you the feelings you have about yourself," she wrote, "It makes you immediately aware of where you are resisting and where you are open and flowing. It clearly shows you what thoughts you will need to change if you want to have a joyous, fulfilling life."

In the beginning, I often notice the discomfort my clients feel when told to look directly in the mirror and say, "You are beautiful, I love you" because they do not believe it.

They feel awkward, they feel inauthentic, they feel silly. But I encourage them to keep doing it anyway even if they do not believe it 100% yet. And I say yet because it usually takes them less than a month to start believing they are beautiful and to start feeling love for themselves.

I'm sure you're familiar with the saying "Fake it until you make it." Well, it isn't really faking, it's simply reconditioning the mind to believe something different than what it's believed for a long time, maybe years.

Remember when you were little and you kissed yourself in the mirror the first time you saw your reflection in it? Yes, reconnect to that time of unapologetic love. You didn't pause to think if you deserve it, you didn't use anyone's beauty standards to decide you were beautiful or not. You just loved yourself the way she was.

The Practice

MIRROR TALK

For the next 30 days, I invite into a journey of relearning to love yourself unconditionally.

Have some privacy and a mirror nearby.

Close your eyes, reconnect to the love that inside you.

Open your eyes. Now look into the mirror, and deep inside your eyes.

Keep looking deeper until you reach your soul,

You will know when you do.

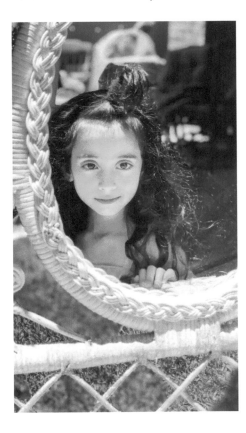

REPEAT

I love you, I really do. You are so special to me.

You are so unique and beautiful the way you are.

If you have difficulty with the statement of unconditional love, substitute it for another one, such as, "You are beautiful in your own unique way" or simply "You are beautiful." Keep repeating it so that your mind starts believing it. This is when you shift your reality and you start seeing your beauty. You'll also start attracting people who appreciate it as well.

Practice Three

MIRROR DANCE THERAPY

Engaging your body in pleasurable activities will set a new tone to your relationship with your body, that's why I believe that mirror dance therapy can create a bond, a connection to your body that you have struggled to accept and love fully.

What is mirror dance therapy?

While dance is a practice of connecting to your body in a pleasurable and self-expressive way, mirror dance is witnessing yourself doing it. When you look at your body in its artistic expression, your body becomes a work of art in progress. No longer is it in a static, passive state but in a flowing, active and variable one.

> *Mirror dance therapy brings more awareness to the multidimensionality of our body and when we start loving some aspects of it, little by little we engage less in hating it, and only then is there hope for a good relationship with our body.*

Mirror dance therapy also helps awakening your inner goddess who has been taught for thousands of years to silence her pleasure and sensuality.

Engaging

YOUR BODY IN PLEASURABLE ACTIVITIES WILL SET A NEW
TONE TO YOUR RELATIONSHIP WITH YOUR BODY,
THAT'S WHY I BELIEVE THAT

Mirror Dance Therapy

CAN CREATE A BOND, A CONNECTION TO YOUR BODY
THAT YOU HAVE STRUGGLED TO ACCEPT AND

Love Fully.

The Practice

MIRROR DANCE THERAPY

Choose an outfit that you see yourself dancing in, in your dreams. It could be a dress, yoga pants or skip the outfit all together (or keep this for later when you feel more comfortable seeing yourself dancing naked, but I highly recommend you do it at some point).

Choose a time and place when you will be uninterrupted for at least 10 minutes and where you have a mirror that shows all of you.

Put on your favorite song or music.

Start dancing freely, let your body move to the music without thinking about right or wrong. It's only you and yourself in the mirror.

It's important to give yourself permission to enjoy moving your body freely without judgment.

Focus on how your body is flowing to the music, how transported and free it feels.

Acknowledge any feelings that may arise.

Take that feeling in your hands and dance with it.

Let's say a feeling of shame arises, externalize it and hold it between your arms, comfort it and dance with it until it dissipates. Don't fight it, see it moving outside your body. This will de-monsterize it so that it can't control you.

Allow whatever feelings of shame, guilt, judgment, inferiority, or embarrassment to arise. Let them move through and out of your body, not by fighting them but rather by soothing them into more love and dancing.

Keep dancing and looking at your self-expression in the mirror, appreciating your body for such a beautiful and enjoyable experience.

Have fun enjoying yourself.

Stop when you have got enough.

Give thanks to your body looking at it in the mirror and saying something like: Thank you, I appreciate you.

FOOD RITUALS

The purpose of a food ritual is to prepare your intention to experience joy and nourishment. In the beginning, food rituals are going to feel awkward and your mind may tell you to skip it, but it is ok to feel weird especially when doing new things. Feel weird and do it anyway.

One   Before you prepare the food, set the intention for nourishment and fuel for your body. Take 3 deep breaths and say internally or out loud:

> *I am setting the intention of preparing food with love and gratitude. This food is going to nourish my body on a deep level. This or something greater, amen.*

Two   Play your favorite music, dance in the kitchen, make it an enjoyable act. All this is going to affect how your food will taste and feel. The more pleasure you feel, the more pleasurable your food will be.

Three   *Have a conversation with your body before you eat (at least at the beginning to undo all the negative thinking and fear linked to food and eating over the years):*

I fully trust you.

You know how to transform any food into nourishment.

I appreciate you for all the things you do so I can enjoy this life.

I am very grateful for you.

I love you.

Food Ritual Affirmations

I FULLY TRUST YOU.

YOU KNOW HOW TO TRANSFORM ANY
FOOD INTO NOURISHMENT.

I APPRECIATE YOU FOR ALL THE THINGS
YOU DO SO I CAN ENJOY THIS LIFE.

I AM VERY GRATEFUL FOR YOU.

I LOVE YOU.

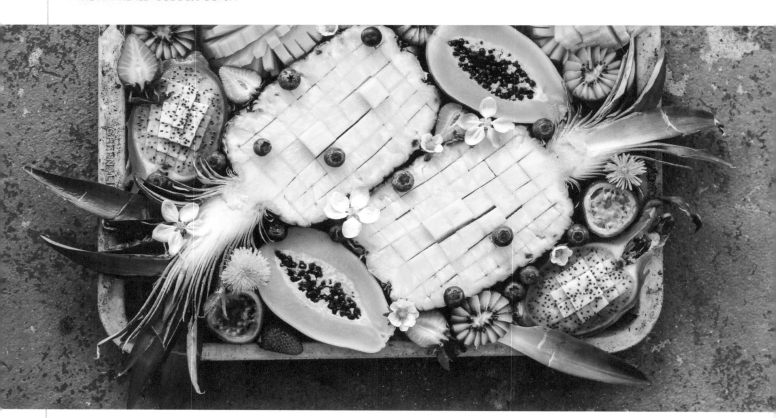

Remember, you can be eating the healthiest food in the world but if you are scared, angry, or have lots of negative feelings while preparing or eating that food, it's going to create negative energy.

Every time you find your mind wandering towards negative thoughts around the food you are about to eat, use the 5-second rule [Practice 5] and change that thought into a positive one.

 Give thanks and appreciation before and after you eat. This is an ancient practice that most of us have lost and it is not arbitrary! People used to pray over the food and give thanks for thousands and thousands of years for a reason—because of the power behind intention. What you give thanks to nourishes you.

Place your hand over the food you are about to eat and say the following:

I appreciate the food on the table.

I set the intention to nourish me on a deep level.

Thank you, God, (or universe) for this food.

Practice Five

THE FIVE-SECOND RULE

During the same period of time I started working out I came upon a book called *The 5-Second Rule* by Mel Robbins. The author describes the simple rule that changed her life (and mine). It consists of a 5-second countdown—Count 5-4-3-2-1 and Go!—to trick your mind to take action without over thinking it.

I use this tool to deal with procrastination, such as when I need to make a phone call or send an email.

My favorite way to use this tool isn't only to take action, however, but rather to catch my negative thoughts and flip them around before they gain momentum.

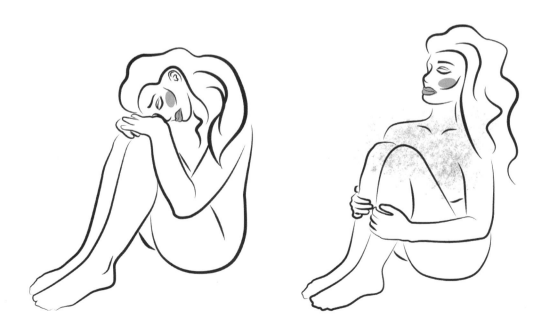

For example, let's say you've decided to change your eating habits and the next day this discouraging thought pops into your mind: "I have tried all kinds of eating regimes and nothing has worked for me, so why is this one going to work now?"

Instead of following the rabbit down the rabbit hole into all the times you've failed and all the disappointments you've felt, you STOP and catch yourself anywhere in that thought and count: 5,4,3,2,1 and shift your thoughts into a positive one, such as:

> *I am now in a different state of mind, I know things will work out for me because now I am approaching my desire [goal] with self-love and self-acceptance, something I have never done before.*
>
> *I know that anything I want to create starts in my mind first.*
> *I see my body in the near future thriving and feeling fit and healthy.*

The 5-second rule is also a super helpful tool for:

1—Conditioning and strengthening the awareness muscle so that you can instantly recognize any negative or self-blaming thought. The more you use it the faster you will become.

2—Stopping those thoughts right before they become uncontrollable and spin-off. It acts like the brakes in the car that prevent you from going down the hill and crashing.

3—Shifting the direction of those thoughts by redirecting them to a higher vibration so you don't get lost in the wrong direction.

Practice Six

BODY MOVEMENT

Have you ever felt like you are stuck in most areas of your life? The feeling that you are not moving forward, you feel paralyzed, uninspired, with no way out? On a physical level, do you feel heavy, disconnected, constipated, irritable, or sluggish?

If you are feeling this way right now, I am here to tell you that you are not alone and that you don't have to feel this way forever. I have been there, and it feels like silent torture. Nothing feels more frustrating than feeling stuck! And when you feel stuck, your body and mind will feel the same.

I have always struggled with the idea of working out, whether to lose weight, create a certain body shape, or achieve health--or because this is what "successful" people do! I used to force myself to work out until I dropped only to find myself, a couple of weeks later, drifting away from it and not wanting to even think about it anymore.

One day, as I was discussing this matter with my husband who is an "alpha" 5 am club kind of person, he said something that shifted my perspective: "I don't feel like working out either before I start, but it makes me feel good once I'm there and after I'm done."

I spent some time thinking about what he said and came to an understanding that helped me to consistently start moving my body.

What I discovered was that associating working out with the immediate gratification of "feeling good" works better than associating it with the long term gratification of "losing weight" or "becoming healthier."

WHAT I DISCOVERED WAS THAT ASSOCIATING WORKING OUT WITH

The Immediate Gratification

OF "FEELING GOOD" WORKS BETTER THAN ASSOCIATING IT WITH THE

Long Term Gratification

OF "LOSING WEIGHT" OR "BECOMING HEALTHIER."

Compare these two attitudes.

Attitude A

I work out because it makes me feel good.

I love feeling the blood pumping through my veins.

I love how energized I instantly feel.

Sweat makes me feel renewed and regenerated.

I love the glow on my face when I'm done, it is like natural botox.

I love the realization of how strong and capable my body can be.

Attitude B

I work out because I want to lose 20 pounds.

I work out to flatten my stomach and build muscle.

I work out to lower my cholesterol or reduce the symptoms of diabetes.

While you may eventually achieve the results of B, it won't happen overnight. In fact, it's going to take months of consistent repetition.

The Practice

BODY MOVEMENT

So what type of work out should you do? I recommend anything that involves moving as the place to start. Whether you dance in your living room, take a walk in the park, put on your running shoes for a jog, or go to your local yoga studio is not as important as being consistent. Fifteen minutes a day is better than 2 hours twice a month.

An immediate benefit for me when I started working out (dancing every day) was an increased flow of energy in my body and mind. I felt more alive and lighter (even though my body weight was the same). The inexplicable pain in my body dissipated, constipation no longer plagued me. It was as if my entire body just started working again.

But what if negative thoughts like self-doubt and self-sabotage start creeping in? Because they will. Then you can try the 5-Second Rule, to help you flip your negative thoughts almost immediately so they can't paralyze you again.

Practice Seven

VISUALIZATIONS (1 & 2)

Visualization One – Energize Your Being

NOTE: This exercise is specifically designed to tap into the flow of your energy and should be done at the beginning of your 7-Day Detox, and at any time you feel the need to increase the flow of your internal energy.

Visualization is something we all do. How many times have you imagined your dream house, that romantic dinner you would like to have with your special someone, the thriving practice where clients are lining up, or the ideal body you absolutely love?

What makes this natural practice effective or not depends on our own beliefs about it: do you think that visualization is just a waste of time or a perfect way to avoid taking action? Or is   it the drafting process of creating and manifesting your dreams?

I belong to the latter group and let me tell you it is quite a miraculous tool because it actually works! Visualizing the things you want in your life will anchor them more in your vibration, will bring them to life, activate them and gives you such a pleasurable experience with no censorship or limitations at all.

Some people doubt the power of visualization because they don't believe that the imagination plays a role in creating reality. But the truth is that the existence of anything starts in your imagination.

The Existence

OF ANYTHING STARTS IN YOUR

Imagination.

Whatever you dream of manifesting, the body, the house, or the career, while you're doing it you're not thinking whether it's logical or realistic, you're just focused on the manifestation, not on the unwanted conditions that are in your face every day. It is the negative focus that keeps *what we don't want* active in our vibration, giving little to no chance for our real desires to come to life.

Let's say you are someone who has been "unlucky" in love, your past relationships are living proof of that. You've gone from one toxic relationship to another to another. One day, an amazing person crosses your path and if you are so focused on your past experience of the unhappy relationships you've had, you miss this new opportunity and thus destroy any hope or chance for this new relationship to enter your life. But if your focus is more on what you want to create instead of on "what is" or "what has always been" then you are free to shift your reality to a new place.

It can be hard to ignore the past, I know but it is possible. So what if today, you give yourself permission to play, to use your imagination as an outlet, allowing yourself to think positive thoughts, be kind to yourself, believe in yourself again and cheer yourself up despite the "reality."

The truth is you are not tied to your history. As an awakened goddess, you are free to create each moment as you want it to be. What we tend to forget is that "reality" is not static! It is not a life sentence, you can change it, not by focusing on it but shifting your attention to its transformation.

This is why I consider visualization to be a powerful tool to create anything you want from wherever you are because where you are doesn't really matter if you are focused on the endpoint. Now, I am not saying, sit there, and dream all day (even though that would be fun to try), what I am saying is use any tool to bring you inspiration and hope and shift your vibration to a positive one so your actions are inspired and not enforced.

> *The healthy, vibrant, fit, radiant body that you want to achieve starts in your mind first! Once you feel how exciting "manifesting that body", "feeling that wellness" or "having that relationship" is, you will be more motivated to do the work so you can get there. Feelings are the most powerful motivators.*

VISUALIZATION 1 — ENERGIZE YOUR BEING

The purpose of this guided meditation and visualization is to activate each chakra with healing energy, facilitate the flow of energy between your energy centers and the universe, and remove any stagnation in your body to allow wellness to flow.

What is a chakra?

Remember how everything is energy? Chakras are energy centers located in your body from the top of the head to the base of your spine. When a chakra is blocked or stagnating, it affects our feelings, organs, behaviors, and health as well as the flow of energy in our body. This guided meditation is intended to recreate balance and flow.

You are going to start by relaxing your body first with deep breathing and then by visualizing a healing light traversing the 7 chakras in your body. (See illustration below.)

Meditation

- Sit in a comfortable position or lay down. Close your eyes, and start breathing deeply, inhaling through your nose and exhaling through your mouth. After a few moments, begin to inhale light and love, and exhale pain and hurt.

- Don't worry if your mind is chattering, you do not need to focus on anything or stop focusing on the things your mind is chattering about, just focus on breathing through it all.

- Feel the way your chest opens naturally. Feel the relaxation sensation. Acknowledge it and bask in it. Notice all the feelings, thoughts and if there is a tension in a particular place in your body, breathe into that area until the tension dissolves. Keep breathing until you feel a deep sense of relaxation.

- Now imagine a big beautiful crystal ball of light coming down from the Universe—God, Divine power, whatever it is you believe in. You don't have to name it.

- This ball of light holds the ultimate divine healing power.

- Imagine the ball glowing into thousands of pure white crystal lights just hanging above your head (*your crown chakra*) feel the warm loving presence of that divine light and welcome it into your awareness. Its presence is reminding you that you are more than just a physical body, you are energy, you are spirit and you have the power to heal your life.

- Allow the light to spin slowly and move down through the top of your head passing through your forehead, in between your eyes (*your third eye chakra*), filling you with a beautiful indigo color, opening your third eye, awakening you to see with the eyes of love and abundance instead of fear and lack.

- Feel the tingling sensation unlocking your fullest potential to see beyond what exists.

- The light changes color and becomes a bright beautiful blue as it moves down your nose, your lips, inside of your mouth, down to your throat, neck, and shoulders. Let it stay there for a while, bathing any stiffness, any tension you may have, and reminding you to speak your truth without disconnecting from your heart. The light flows from one shoulder to another, going through your neck and throat (*your throat chakra*), bathing your muscles with inner wisdom and truth of who you are: an eternal being.

- The light moves to your heart area (*your heart chakra*) morphing into a gorgeous emerald color bringing more hope and life to your heart and reminding you of your endless source of love and abundance. You are love and you are loved infinitely.

- Your heart and lungs are immersed in that shimmery green light opening your heart to more compassion towards yourself and others and washing away resentment, judgment, and any hatred that may be shutting down your power.

- As the light moves down to your gut area (*solar plexus chakra*), it starts glowing in a beautiful sunny yellow color that activates the fire within you, waking up your dormant energy and fueling you with the power to change. This beautiful golden light goes through your liver, decongesting it from anger, frustration and irritability that may be stored there.

- The light is then passed to your intestines bathing your cells with divine light, healing your gut on a cellular level, reactivating your digestive fire and your body's ability to transform food into nutrients, ideas into projects, and inspiration into action that your body needs to thrive.

- Right now this light is dissipating any worries, fear, obsessions, fixation, anxiety around the food that you are eating and any thought that you are not enough or incapable. The light is reminding your cells that they are powerful, they are loved, they are appreciated for the work they are doing.

- If you are experiencing any bloating, indigestion, gas, sensitivity, intolerance, tenderness, constipation, blockage, stagnation, worry, insecurity, anxiety, see it now being carried away or dissolved by the light. Your gut area is now shining with that bright golden light and making you feel confident in its power.

- The light keeps traveling through your body and when it gets below your navel (*your sacral chakra*), it changes into a comforting warm orange and circulates through your kidneys, reproductive organs and your bowels igniting your creative energy, your right to feel pleasure and the joy of being in the flow of life.

- Any sexual trauma, any feelings of shame, guilt, hurt, fear is being healed right now by that beautiful ball of orange light transcending your past hurtful experiences into a learning experience of compassion and healing.

- The orange light goes deeper and deeper to where it hurts the most, dissipating any pain with its divine power, reminding you that you can heal your life, and give away your pain to a higher power.

- Feel that pain leaving your body, transported in that glowing ball of light that now changes into a beautiful ruby red, glowing at the base of your spine (*your root chakra*), healing any back pain or feeling of being unsupported or insecure, providing you with the trust that you are always being taken care of. It goes down your legs and roots you deeply into the earth.

- Imagine your feet growing red roots that extend deep, deep down into the earth and transporting that ball out of your body and into the center of the earth, removing all the blockages, toxins and anything else that no longer serves you. The earth recycles the ball of light back into the universe into that crystal white light of purity and grace that fills the whole universe.

- Take a deep breath feeling the ball of light going down deep into the earth and leaving you filled with pristine white crystal light, inside and all around you, you are now glowing with divine light growing so big that it is illuminating the whole universe. Feel the oneness with the universe. Feel the power within you to heal yourself and the whole universe.

- Your body is now healed, your body is now free and forever aware of the availability of that divine light to keep the flow of life active within you and to transform your pain into power.

- Keep breathing into that image of white crystal pristine light of oneness and healing.

Come back when you are ready.

Notice how you feel.

Give thanks

VISUALIZATIONS (1 & 2)

Visualization Two – Create Your Ideal Body

Sit in a quiet place (or lay down, I recommend doing this exercise at night when laying down in bed just before falling asleep)

Close your eyes.
Center yourself.

Relax your body by taking a couple of deep breaths.

Bring awareness to the power of your imagination in creating any image you desire.

Now see your Ideal Self, in your ideal shape, weight. See the conditions, situation, day, place, weather, and company (if any).

Give as much details as possible:

Where are you?

Are you with someone? If yes, who?

What are you wearing?

How does your body look? (Give as many details as possible)
Describe your shape, muscles, weight, posture, hair, face, skin, voice, arms, chest, belly, thighs, and legs, describe everything you see using what a positive adjective, such as: toned, strong, smooth, radiant, glowing, fit, on point, shiny, curvy, skinny, sexy, slim, rounded, gained weight or lost weight.

What are you doing?

How are you feeling?

Now stay there for a while, feel all those feelings of exhilaration, excitement, joy, satisfaction, pleasure, contentment, attractiveness, sexiness, and aliveness.

Enjoy savoring those feelings, bathing in the amazing pleasure they're giving you, take your time.

Now, gather all those feelings into a good feelings box that you store in a safe place near your heart.

Place your right hand on your heart and feel them, they are with you now, they are yours, always there in that box, in your heart, a place you can come back to any time you want to anticipate what is coming, what is going to manifest, just the way you imagined it.

Smile, come back and open your eyes when you are ready.

Draw your body manifestation below.

Practice Eight

APPRECIATION JOURNAL

Another practice that changed my life and the life of my clients is cultivating an appreciation for all that is by recording what you are grateful for in your journal on a regular basis.

When we are in a state of appreciation, we surrender control of how things should be and start seeing the beauty in all things as they are.

We can stop being attached to how our body should be or look like and start focusing on all the things our body is and does for us, no matter how small or big. The more you appreciate what you see, encounter, have, and experience, the more you call upon things, situations, experiences and people to grow and expand in their abundance.

You don't need a lot to practice appreciation, from the comfort of your favorite chair to the air that you breathe and the birds singing outside, from the flowers dancing in the breeze, to the food on the table, or a smile from a stranger. Just look around you and appreciate every single thing as it is,

The law is simple and is universal, whatever energy you focus upon and activate you will get in return.

Appreciation

WHEN WE ARE IN A STATE OF
APPRECIATION, WE SURRENDER
CONTROL OF HOW THINGS SHOULD
BE AND START SEEING THE BEAUTY IN
ALL THINGS AS THEY ARE.

The Practice

APPRECIATION JOURNAL

Reasons that journaling your appreciation is a great practice, especially at the beginning of your day:

1—First, journaling is a practice of becoming present with yourself, something most of miss out on these days. It only takes 5 or 10 minutes, just enough to set the tone for the rest of the day.

2—Writing is a powerful tool that gives us a physical connection to our ideas, thoughts, and feelings. We can see them, read them and hold them in our hand. How many times do you get an inspiring idea that you forget because you didn't write it down on paper? Writing down our desires and goals also has the power to give them life!

3—When you focus journaling your appreciation, you are bringing awareness to the multitude and infinite things you are can appreciate and as a result, you are realizing how much there is in life to appreciate. You are raising your vibration from lack to abundance, from control to contentment, from fear to trust, from hate to love.

I invite you to start your day with writing for 5 to 10 minutes in your appreciation journal.

- *I appreciate waking up to a brand-new day where I get to experience a day that I have never lived before with all the things I get to experience, the people I get to meet and the new things I get to learn.*

- *I appreciate being alive and able to create my life one thought at a time.*

- *I appreciate the smell of coffee brewing in my coffee machine, getting ready for me to taste and enjoy.*

- *I appreciate my body's ability to breathe and keep me alive while I was sleeping.*

- *I appreciate my body movement and the freedom I have to navigate through the day. (and for someone who has lost this privilege, it can go like this: I appreciate the people who help me get out of bed and dress me and this wheelchair that gives me the freedom to go to places).*

- *I appreciate the baker next door and the aroma of the freshly baked bread.*

- *I appreciate all the people walking on the street going to their job or starting their day and keeping me company without even knowing.*

- *I appreciate the birds, dogs and all animal life around me which reminds me that life can be experienced in so many different ways.*

- *I appreciate the flowers that grow without waiting for anything in return ad that brightens my days with their beauty and fragrance.*

- *I appreciate my eyes for being able to witness this miracle of life, my ears for hearing all the music, my touch for the tactile experience, my smell for all the pleasing olfactory memories I get to store and come back to, my taste for all the different culinary experiments I get to savor.*

- *I appreciate a helping hand from a stranger opening the door for me, a smile from an old woman who reminds me that the ultimate goal of life is happiness.*

- *I appreciate the traffic lights for making driving and walking such a harmonious coexistence.*

- *I appreciate the mailman for delivering my packages, the garbage truck for taking my trash, the sun for shining and the earth for providing oxygen and water and hanging in the space without falling.*

BODY APPRECIATION PRACTICE

Choose a feature that you love about yourself and appreciate it: I appreciate my beautiful eyes or nose or lips or hips or legs or eyebrows or how my back is shaped or my toes, or hair, anything that you see as beautiful in yourself.

I appreciate my body for keeping me alive.

I appreciate my body for giving me this physical experience of flesh, blood, bones and features that are unique to me.

I appreciate all the work my body does without me intervening like pumping blood through my veins, digesting the food I eat and transforming it into nourishment and fuel, breathing, filtering waste, creating movement, touching, smelling, seeing, hearing and sleeping at night for rest.

I appreciate that my body is so resilient it could survive surgeries, pregnancies, heartbreaks, and injuries.

I appreciate how my body always works in my favor and when it doesn't, it is sending me messages so I can clear any blocked energy and get into alignment.

When you state your love or appreciation for at least one part of your body, your subconscious will receive this as a love note towards your whole body, it will not differentiate between the cells of your nose or your eyes, and as the love is received, your whole body is going to benefit.

When you make the unwavering intention to start loving yourself, your whole being will contribute to making it happen. Just start with what you have, with what you like and focus on it, send it love, talk to it nicely; your whole body will be listening and will respond accordingly.

Part III

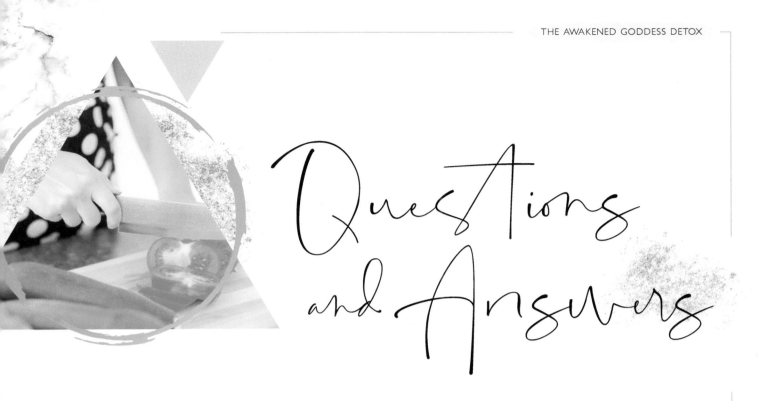

Questions and Answers

How will I get the greatest benefit from this detox?

1. Follow the 7 days of menus and stick to eating all the high vibrational foods prepared with wholesome ingredients and drinking water as suggested—unless, of course, you have food allergies or a medical condition that prohibits your eating certain foods. [See the List of Ingredients.]

2. Keep your thoughts and feelings positive by using the Practices. Start two weeks before as well as during the food detox to prepare the vibration for your body and mind to yield better and lasting results.

3. Spend at least 15 minutes in Nature (outdoors) every day.

4. Keep your body flowing with the Mirror Dance practice and any other physical exercise you prefer.

When should I do this detox?

Certainly, fall and spring are ideal times for detox and cleansing, but since this is a very gentle detox and not limited to food detox, it can be done any time of year. You will not be depriving yourself, you will not feel hungry, and you won't have to force yourself to eat food that is not enjoyable. You will eat more vegetables, fruits, nuts, beans and whole grains like quinoa. Just don't do the detox during the week you have 2 birthdays and 3 weddings!

What kind of prep do I need to do?

Shop for the ingredients ahead of time, according to how busy your lifestyle is. If you are a working mom, I recommend you get all the ingredients on Saturday for a Monday start, keeping them for each day in a separate bag or box or on a particular shelf of the fridge or pantry. If you have more time, you may want to go shopping every other day or the day before.

Besides the comprehensive **List of Ingredients**, you will be provided with the shopping list for each day plus a reminder on the day before if anything needs be soaked or prepared ahead of time, which is very minimal in this program.

Are there substitutes provided for the ingredients?

Yes, a substitution list is included with the **List of Ingredients**.

Can the whole family eat with me?

Absolutely! These recipes are made with whole food ingredients that everybody can eat. That's why some of the recipes have 2 or 3 servings. It's motivating and fun to do this detox with your family and not have to worry about having to cook for them separately.

What do I do with leftovers?

If you're doing the detox alone, you may have leftovers which will keep very well for several days. And yes, you can freeze any leftover of these recipes for up to three months, just make sure it's in a sealed container.

Should I follow the menus in the order presented, or can I change their sequence?

It's important, for the first week, to follow these recipes in the exact order. These recipes and the way I prepared, tested and photographed them was almost channeled, as if it wasn't really me doing the work, but a greater force guiding me for the highest good of all. After the first week is done, feel free to follow the order you like.

Can I skip meals?

I don't recommend you skip meals unless you don't feel like eating at all. Otherwise, follow the order of meals as presented for the seven days.

Can I skip snacks?

I do recommend you snack only if you feel hungry between meals. If not, you can totally skip snacking. Snacks are very easy to prepare and require 2 to 3 minutes to fix.

When should I eat meals?

It really depends on your lifestyle. Here are some options.

- **First option**
  Breakfast: 7 am
  Lunch: 12 pm
  Dinner: 5 pm

- **Second option**
  Breakfast: 8 am
  Lunch: 1 pm
  Dinner: 6 pm

- **Third option**
  Breakfast: 9 am
  Lunch: 2 pm
  Dinner: 7 pm

- Snack in between meals. For example, if you eat breakfast at 7 am and lunch at 12 pm, your first snack will be around 10 am.

How much water do I need to drink every day? And when is the best time to drink water?

Room temperature water is a huge part of this detox. Follow these guidelines for your water intake:

- *500 ml on an empty stomach (2 cups or 16 fl. oz.)*
- *250 ml one hour after breakfast (1 cup or 8 fl. oz.)*
- *250 ml + squeeze of lemon juice one hour before lunch ((1 cup or 8 fl. oz.)*
- *250 ml 1 hour after lunch ((1 cup or 8 fl. oz.)*
- *250 ml + squeeze of lemon juice one hour before dinner (1 cup or 8 fl. oz.)*
- *250 ml 1 hour after dinner (1 cup or 8 fl. oz.)*
- *250 ml 1 hour before bedtime (1 cup or 8 fl. oz.)*

How much weight can I expect to lose?

It really depends on each person and how much extra weight they are carrying. I urge you to consider weight loss as a bonus not as a goal in itself, first, because focusing less on the weight will make it happen faster, second, because each person is different, and third, results will depend on how closely you follow the menu and maintain a high vibration, and how consistent you are with the Practices.

What can I do to stay on track after the 7 days are over?

Most people feel lost after they finish a detox or a diet plan. That's the great thing about this detox approach! Because you will be eating whole nourishing and satisfying foods, you will not have to reintroduce food slowly like in other strict protocols. Just continue to focus on whole foods and supporting your high vibration.

Now even though the recipes in this book are 100% plant-based, this program is for everybody. After the first week of eating plant-based food you may not wish to go back to eating meat every single day and that is normal because you will feel the shift in your energy.

Some of you may feel drawn to a mostly plant-based diet or return to your former routine.

In all cases, I recommend several guidelines if you want to maintain a healthy lifestyle

See Guidelines on the next page

Guidelines

Eat a variety of vegetables, get inspired by
the recipes in this book.

Eat fresh and seasonal fruits.

Drink more water.

Be more mindful about your animal product intake
and keep it to a minimum.

Notice how different foods make you feel
and eat accordingly.

Keep doing the affirmations to help you change
your negative beliefs to positive ones.

Keep trusting your body, by supporting your health and vitality with
food that is the closest to Mother Nature.

Laugh and play more.

Get adequate sleep (7 to 8 hours) and respect
your circadian rhythm, sleeping at night and
waking around sunrise.

Allow your body to take a break from food at least
for 10 to 12 hours at night.

Move that body, dance more.

Do things you love, try a new hobby.

Connect to the love in your heart.

Let go of what is no longer serving you.

Spend time in Nature.

Practice gratitude.

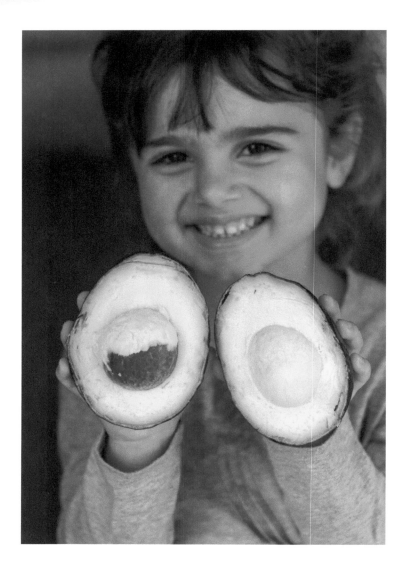

Can I repeat the 7-day detox the following week?

Of course, you can. Feel free to follow the order of days or meals, mix and match meals from different days and create a whole new menu for the week. (if you have leftovers then you may be almost all set for week 2.) You can also use the substitutions (check substitution list) to have more variety.

If you return to your eating routine, be mindful of the processed and refined foods as much as possible like white sugar, white flour, white pasta, white rice, artificial ingredients, junk/fast food. The best way to do this is by adding more high vibrational food. One suggestion would be to eat at least one meal a day of choice from the 7 days detox menu.

The detox program consists of 7 affirmations, 21 recipes, and 7 (14) snacks. Prep, cooking time and the number of servings are provided with the recipes. You will also find a day-by-day shopping list to set up your detox for success.

Before every meal, use the affirmation given for each day to set your positive intention.

THE DAY BEFORE

> *NOTE: Before you begin, go to Practice 7 and do Visualization 1. This exercise is specifically designed to tap into the flow of your energy and can be done at any time you feel the need to increase your internal energy.*

The day before you start your 7 days detox, soak the following nuts and seeds to use as toppings or to snack on between meals as needed. Soaking nuts and seeds will activate them and make them more digestible and more delicious!

Soak
1 cup of almonds.
1 cup of walnuts
1 cup of pistachios
½ cup of sunflower seeds
¼ cup pine nuts (optional)

Soak the nuts in separate bowls at room temperature for 24 hours, changing the water they are soaking in once a day. After 24 hours, add clean water again and keep them refrigerated until serving time.

Day One

SET THE INTENTION

Affirmation

Repeat with every meal.

- *Look at your food and give thanks.*

- *Close your eyes, place your hand on your heart, connect to the love within you.*

- *Take 5 deep breaths as follows: Take a deep breath, counting to 5 for the inhale, hold your breath, count to 3, and exhale, counting to 7.*

- *Place the palm of your hand on above your food and say this affirmation out loud 5 times:*

- *I set the intention for this food to deeply nourish and support my body.*

- *Notice how you feel. Smile. Eat with enjoyment.*

Breakfast
GREEN GODDESS SMOOTHIE

Preparation time: 10 minutes | Servings: 1

If you are not a big fan of kale or any other ingredient but are a fan of its health benefits, one guaranteed solution for you (and your kids): sneak it in a smoothie!

This green smoothie is inspired by a Lebanese fruit cocktail I grew up eating based on avocado, milk, and honey and topped with all kinds of fruits and soaked nuts.

I just tweaked it a ma manière and I promise you will love it, if my kids did, then you surely will.

I kept the sweetener to a minimum though, because remember we are on a gentle detox.

Ingredients

2 kale leaves, de-stemmed (or ¼ cup of spinach)

2 super-ripe frozen bananas (approx. 1 ½ cup of frozen banana chunks)

1 cup unsweetened almond or coconut milk

1 tbsp. hemp seeds

½ pitted medium size avocado

1 tbsp. fresh lemon juice

1 tbsp. maple syrup

Tiny pinch of sea salt

Toppings

½ cup sliced strawberries (4 big strawberries)

1 tbsp. soaked almonds.

1 tbsp. soaked pistachios

1 tsp. cacao nibs

Mint leaves for garnish

Directions

1. Add milk, kale leaves, avocado, lemon juice, maple syrup & sea salt to a high-speed blender, and blend until smooth and creamy.
2. Add frozen bananas & blend again until smooth.
3. Serve in a bowl.
4. Add the toppings and enjoy!

Snack
FANCY CARROT STICKS

Preparation time: 10 minutes | Servings: 1

Believe it or not, this snack is exactly the same one my dad used to have with his scotch on a Friday night! Yes, in Lebanon, we serve this snack with alcohol. It's called balance. It is satisfying, super delicious and nutritious; it is also a new way to look at snacking.

Beta carotene, yes, please!

Ingredients

2 carrots, cut into batonnets
½ lemon, juiced
Pinch of sea salt

Directions

1. Wash your carrots and peel them.
2. Cut into batonnets or any shape you prefer.
3. Transfer to a shallow bowl.
4. Add lemon juice and salt.
5. Enjoy.

If it is easier for you just to eat the carrot as is, feel free to do that. I am just giving you the most delicious way to do it.

Lunch
MOUJADDARA & CABBAGE SALAD

Moujaddara or lentil purée and rice is one of my favorite Lebanese dishes that almost every house in Lebanon makes on Friday, as a reminiscence of good Friday when we do not eat any animal products. Packed with plant-based protein, and paired with cabbage salad, this dish is comforting and nutritious. Did I mention I ditched the white rice for quinoa? Can we please stop obsessing about protein?

MOUJADDARA

Preparation time: 10 minutes | Cooking Time: 60 minutes
Total Time: 1 hr 10 minutes | Servings: 2

Ingredients

1 medium yellow onion, cut in 4 quarters
1 cup of brown lentils, soaked with a pinch of sea salt for 2 hours if possible
3 cups of water
½ tsp. cumin powder
¾ tsp. sea salt
Pinch of black pepper
2 tbsp. quinoa
2 tbsp. olive oil

Directions

1. Add the onions, drained lentils, water, cumin powder, black pepper & sea salt in a pot and bring to a boil on high heat, uncovered.
2. Lower the heat, cover the pot and let simmer for 45 minutes.
3. **NOTE**: While the Moujaddara is cooking, prepare the Cabbage Salad.
4. After the lentils have cooked, use an immersion blender and blend really well until creamy and smooth.
5. Make sure the immersion blender lower part is fully immersed in the mixture while blending to prevent splashing the kitchen with the lentils mixture.
6. Add 2 tbsp of quinoa, bring to a boil again then let simmer for 10 minutes on low heat, covered.
7. Turn off the heat.
8. Adjust salt to taste, you may add up to ¼ tsp.
9. Stir in olive oil and serve.

Cabbage is an amazing detoxifier, anti-inflammatory agent and rich in fiber! It also makes a delicious salad that you will fall in love with especially because it involves massage! Did I mention you can eat the whole thing?

CABBAGE SALAD

Preparation time: 15 minutes | Servings: 4

Ingredients

1 small cabbage head, rinsed and drained
1 ripe tomato, cut into cubes

Dressing

1 clove of garlic, crushed in a mortar
2 tbsp. olive oil
¼ cup fresh lemon juice (approx. 2 to 3 lemons)
½ tsp. sea salt
½ tsp. dried mint

Directions

1. Shred the cabbage finely using a mandolin or if not available, using a sharp knife.
2. Transfer to a big bowl.
3. In a small bowl, whisk together all the dressing ingredients until well combined.
4. I prefer to use a small jar with a lid and shake well before pouring over the salad.
5. Pour over the cabbage in the big bowl.
6. Use your hands to massage to cabbage and give it some love and nourishment with your good intentions.
7. Massage for 2 minutes or until the cabbage has softened.
8. Add the tomatoes and give it a mix.
9. This salad tastes better if refrigerated for 15 minutes prior to eating.
10. Have one plate of moujaddara (1 ½ or 2 cups max) with the whole salad or until satisfied.
11. Stir in olive oil and serve.

HOT GRANNY

There is something about preparing food as simple as an apple that makes it more appealing and creates a different experience around it.

Cayenne pepper is an excellent metabolism booster and when paired with tart or sweet acidic apple, it balances the flavors in an interesting way.

Preparation time: 5 minutes | Servings: 1

Ingredients

1 Granny Smith apple cut into slices
Pinch of cayenne pepper

Directions

1. Wash the apple.
2. Cut in half.
3. Remove the seeds.
4. Slice it and sprinkle with a pinch of cayenne pepper.

AVOCADO ON SWEET POTATO TOAST

Growing up, I wasn't really a fan of sweet potatoes, we don't eat them much in Lebanon, and when I first tried it, I had mixed feelings, like is it sweet or savory? Until I came up with this recipe which is flavorful, colorful and rich, a real pleasure for your senses.

Lots of beta carotene in one day is never a bad idea! (Think anti-oxidation, anti-inflammation, skin rejuvenation and immunity.)

Preparation time: 10 minutes | Cooking time: 25 minutes
Total time: 35 minutes | Servings: approx. 6 sweet potato toasts

Ingredients

1 sweet potato, cut into ½ inch slice
Avocado oil to brush the sweet potato slices
Pinch of sea salt
Pinch of black pepper
Pinch of dried mint (or dried herb of choice)

1 big ripe avocado
½ lime, juiced
Pinch of sea salt
Pinch of red pepper flakes

2 tsp. avocado oil
1 clove of garlic, finely minced
2 tbsp. pine nuts
1 cup sliced fresh mushrooms (approx. 4 oz)
6 baby artichokes, cut in quarters

Garnish
Squeeze of lime
Fresh mint leaves

Directions

1. Preheat the oven at 400 F.
2. Wash the sweet potato well.
3. Cut it into ½ inch slices (skin on) and place on a baking tray & brush with oil.
4. Sprinkle with sea salt, black pepper and dried mint.
5. Bake at 400 F for 20 minutes, then broil for 2 minutes & turn off the oven.
6. Heat in a non-stick a medium skillet on medium heat. Add the pine nuts and sauté until golden brown about 30 sec, stirring frequently to prevent the nuts from burning.
7. Transfer to a small bowl.
8. In the same skillet, heat 1 tsp of oil then add minced garlic and sauté for 30 sec on low to medium heat, stirring frequently.
9. Add the mushrooms and sauté on medium heat until golden brown, for about 5 minutes.
10. Do not add any salt while cooking the mushrooms.
11. Transfer to a bowl.
12. Drain the artichoke hearts, cut them in quarters and sauté them briefly in the same skillet.
13. In a plate, mash the avocado using a fork, add 1 tbsp lime juice and a pinch of salt & red pepper flakes.

Assembly

1. Spread some mashed avocado on each sweet potato toast.
2. Top with sautéed mushrooms, artichokes and pine nuts.
3. Add a pinch of black pepper, a squeeze of lime and garnish with fresh mint leaves and edible flowers (if using any).
4. Enjoy!

Day Two

TRUST

Affirmation

Repeat with every meal.

- *I relax and enjoy my food knowing that my body is an expert at transforming this food into fuel, energy and nourishment. I fully trust my body.*

- *Relaxing allows my body to do its job without resistance and stress.*

Congratulations! You made it to day 2! Give yourself a tap on the shoulder and get ready for another delicious day as you allow yourself to open further to the experience!

Breakfast
ROSE-SCENTED CHIA PUDDING PARFAIT

Preparation time: 5 minutes | Setting time: 25 minutes
Total time: 30 minutes | Servings: 1

This breakfast is delicious, it almost feels like a dessert, and the best thing about it is that it can be prepared the night before, you can take it with you to work and it will still taste amazing.

Chia seeds, don't get fooled how tiny they look, these little seeds have superpowers thanks to their omega-3 and protein-packed content! They are also loaded with fiber which is great if you want to feel full until your next meal.

Ingredients

To make the chia pudding
¼ cup chia seeds
1 cup unsweetened plant-based milk of choice
2 tbsp. maple syrup
1 tsp. rose water - Rose water is commonly found in Middle Eastern stores but you can also order it online and find it at other health food stores.

Raspberry yogurt
½ cup unsweetened plant-based yogurt of choice
½ cup raspberries
1 tsp. maple syrup

Toppings

Fresh raspberries
1 tbsp crushed pistachios (or any nut of choice)
1 tbsp shredded coconut

Directions

1. Start by preparing the chia pudding by stirring the chia seeds in the milk with the maple syrup and rose water in a medium bowl.
2. Place in the fridge until it sets.
3. Meanwhile, blend together yogurt, raspberries and maple syrup.
4. When the pudding is on the firm side and the chia seeds have expanded (usually takes around 30 minutes) assemble your parfait as follows:
5. You can use a plate or a cup, start with the chia pudding, add the yogurt mixture and garnish with your favorite toppings.

Snack
COOKED BEET WITH SEA SALT

Cooking time: 30 minutes | Servings: 2

Beets are liver's best friends! They support the natural process of detoxification in the body. If you are talking detox, beets should be involved!

A host to a multitude of minerals, vitamins, anti-oxidants and more, beets being a root vegetable, help ground us and balance our root chakra.

As the saying goes: breathe properly, stay curious and eat your beets.

Ingredients

4 medium-size beets
Enough water to cover
Pinch of salt

Directions

1. Wash the beets to remove any dirt.
2. Add them to a medium pot and add enough water to cover them.
3. Add a pinch of sea salt, bring to a boil.
4. Reduce heat to low and let simmer, covered for 30 minutes or until a fork is inserted easily.
5. Drain.
6. Peel one beet cut it into pieces and sprinkle with a tiny pinch of sea salt.
7. Keep the other beets in a bowl, covered, in the fridge for tomorrow's beet salad.

GLUTEN-FREE TAGLIATELLE WITH BASIL-SCENTED MAYO

Because this is not a harsh detox, you won't feel deprived, or obsess over counting calories. It is all about eating highly nutritious food, therefore the pasta I am using here is made of brown rice and isn't just empty calories, and the sauce is made of avocados, tahini, garlic and basil, all foods good at aiding the body in the natural detoxification process.

Did I mention it is also comforting, filling and delicious?!

For those of you who like zucchini noodles, also known as zoodles, there is an option to substitute the brown rice pasta with zucchini noodles.

Preparation time: 7 minutes | Cooking Time: 10 minutes
Total Time: 17 minutes | Servings for the sauce: 3

Ingredients

For the pasta, if you are only cooking 4oz per 1 serving; if you are cooking the whole package: 3 servings)

4oz brown rice tagliatelle (or you can cook the whole package if more people are eating with you).

If you don't want to use pasta, you can substitute any vegetable that you can spiralize like large zucchinis, beets, combining as many as you like. You will also need to get a spiralizer.

For the sauce
1 ripe avocado, pitted and peeled
2 tbsp. tahini paste
1 lemon, juiced
1 tsp. sea salt
¼ cup fresh basil leaves
2 cloves of garlic, peeled
2 tbsp. olive oil
½ cup cherry tomatoes, cut in half

Directions

1. First, cook your pasta according to the directions on the package.
2. If you are using veggies instead of pasta, wash your veggie and spiralize it or you can find vegetables already spiralized in many health food stores.
3. Transfer them to a bowl, add the black pepper, toss and set aside.
4. While the pasta is cooking, prepare the sauce.

To make the sauce

1. Blend together: lemon juice, avocado, garlic, basil and salt.
2. Add the oil by streaming a fine line through the blender until the sauce is completely smooth and emulsified.
3. You may need to stop the blender, scrape down the sides and blend again.
4. Be patient with the blending process to get the best results.
5. If using veggies, especially zucchini, do not add salt ahead of time or mix it with the sauce long time before serving or else all the water content in the zucchini will make the sauce watery and runny. Just add the sauce when ready to serve.
6. To serve, toss 1½ cup of pasta with 4 tbsp of sauce.
7. Add a pinch of black pepper, basil leaves and cherry tomatoes.
8. Enjoy.

SACRED DATES

Long before science depicted the numerous benefits of dates, these magical fruits were considered to have healing properties since Biblical times. They are mentioned 50 times in the Bible and 20 times in the Quran. (Date palm: Wikipedia) They were also considered a symbol of abundance, fertility, health, prosperity and triumph.

If you are not a big fan, I recommend you try this snack, you will fall hard for them, I am sure!

Preparation time: 5 minutes | Servings: 1

Ingredients

3 medjool dates (or any other type)
3 soaked almonds
2 tsp. pomegranate seeds
Cinnamon

Directions

1. Remove the pit and fill each date with 1 soaked almond on one side and pomegranate seeds on the other side. Fold back.
2. Sprinkle with cinnamon. Enjoy!

Dinner

PROTEIN LETTUCE BOATS

One of my favorites! Light and filling at the same time, with lots of textures, colors and flavors, and it only requires 30 minutes to makes, I am sure you will also become a fan!

As for the sauce, it is a Lebanese dressing that we usually eat with falafel and it is called Tarator.

Preparation time: 30 minutes | Assembly time: 3 minutes
Total time: 33 minutes | Servings: 6 boats or 2 to 3 servings

Ingredients

1 head of butter lettuce, rinsed and drained (or any kind of lettuce) and separated into individual leaves
1 can of kidney beans, rinsed and drained
2 tbsp. avocado oil
2 cloves of garlic, minced
1 cup of fresh mushrooms, peeled and sliced
1 cup of organic corn
1 tbsp. liquid aminos (or shoyu or soy sauce)
Pinch of cumin powder

½ cup grape tomatoes, cut in halves
1 avocado, pitted, peeled and diced
Fresh mint leaves

For the tarator sauce

½ cup of tahini
1/3 cup lemon juice
½ tsp. sea salt
¼ cup water to thin
cayenne pepper to taste

Directions

1. Preheat a skillet with 2 tbsp of avocado oil on medium heat.
2. Add the garlic and sauté briefly (for 30 sec), stirring frequently.
3. Add the mushrooms and sauté until golden brown.
4. Add the beans with a pinch of cumin and sauté for 1 minute.
5. Add liquid aminos (shoyu or soy sauce), give it a stir and let it simmer for 3 minutes on medium heat.
6. Lower the heat, add the corn and let simmer for 10 minutes.

Meanwhile, make the tarator

1. In a medium bowl, mix together tahini, lemon juice, salt and cayenne pepper.
2. Add water, little by little, to thin to desired consistency. Don't worry if it looks crumbly at the beginning, it will thin out, just keep mixing with water until smooth. It should be creamy and pourable.

Assembly

1. Arrange your lettuce leaves on a serving board or plate and fill each one with 2 to 3 tbsp of the beans, corn & mushrooms mixture.
2. Top with grape tomatoes, avocados and fresh mint leaves.
3. Dress with tarator to taste.

Day Three

APPRECIATE

Affirmation

Repeat with every meal.

- *I fully love and accept my body. I am so grateful for all the things my body does for me without my intervention: breathing, my heart beating, cell regeneration, digestion and more.*

- *I let my body do its job with ease and grace.*

OATMEAL PUDDING

Preparation time: 5 minutes | Cooking time: 10 minutes
Total time: 15 minutes | Servings: 2

I created this kid-approved recipe after my second daughter was born. I was craving something called Cerelac, an instant cereal made from wheat, milk powder and sugar! I used to LOVE it. This warm breakfast satisfied those childhood cravings in a healthier way using only 3 main ingredients: oats, dates and water! Leftovers can be refrigerated in single-serving cups as pudding to enjoy later with fruits and other toppings.

Ingredients

1 cup rolled oats
2 and ½ cups water
8 medjool dates, pitted
Pinch of cinnamon
Small pinch of sea salt

Toppings

1 tbsp. soaked pistachios
1 blood orange, peeled and sliced
1 tbsp almond butter
1 tbsp. unsweetened shredded coconut
1 tsp. cacao nibs

Directions

1. Add all the ingredients to a small pot or saucepan, bring to a boil and then let it cook, covered, on low heat for 15 minutes.
2. Using an immersion blender, blend until smooth and creamy.
3. Serve and top with soaked nuts, fresh berries and a tablespoon of nut butter.
4. (You can add seeds, raisins, cacao nibs, shredded coconut as well.)

Snack

BASIL-WRAPPED WATERMELON BALLS

Preparation time: 10 minutes | Servings: 2

A refresher for the palette and cooler for the body. Balancing today's breakfast, watermelon is a natural diuretic helping the body get rid of excess fluids that the body is holding on.

Did you know that Watermelon is part fruit, part vegetable?

Or that the green rind is completely edible with so many health benefits. If your watermelon has seeds, eat them too, they are rich in zinc, protein, iron and fiber.

Ingredients

Half a small watermelon
Basil leaves
Black pepper

Directions

1. Using a melon scooper, scoop out watermelon balls.
2. Wrap each ball with a basil leaf. Secure with a toothpick.
3. Sprinkle black pepper.
4. Enjoy!

Lunch
CHICKPEA QUINOA SALAD

Salads don't have to sound, look or taste boring anymore! And most importantly leave you starving and wishing you could eat anything you can get your hands on. This salad is my to-go meal on days when I do not have time to cook, have some quinoa leftovers and want to provide a nourishing and high protein meal for me and my family.

Preparation time: 10 minutes | Cooking Time: 12 minutes
Assembly time: 3 minutes | Total Time: 25 minutes | Servings: 1

Ingredients

To cook the quinoa
1 cup quinoa
1 ¾ cups water
Pinch of sea salt

1 avocado, pitted, peeled and sliced
1 cucumber, diced
1 cup baby arugula (or any greens of choice)
½ cup cooked chickpeas
1 tbsp. hemp hearts
½ cup grape tomatoes
7 pitted olives, sliced

Dressing
1 lemon, juiced
1 tbsp. liquid aminos (or tamari)
1 tbsp. olive oil
Pinch of sea salt
1/8 tsp. black pepper

Directions

1. Whisk all the dressing ingredients together in a small bowl.
2. Set aside.

To cook the quinoa

1. Rinse the quinoa with fresh water, drain and add to a medium-size pot with water and salt.
2. Bring to a boil on high heat, uncovered, then lower the heat and cook, covered, for 13 minutes. Turn off the heat and let sit for 5 minutes.
3. Transfer 1 cup of cooked quinoa to a bowl to cool a bit.
4. You are only going to use 1 cup of cooked quinoa for this recipe and will have 2½ cups of leftovers that you are going to use in other recipes, keep the leftover quinoa in a sealed container in the fridge.

Assembly

1. Add all the salad ingredients to a big bowl.
2. Add the sauce, toss and serve.
3. Keep any leftovers in a closed container in the fridge.
4. Also keep the leftovers of quinoa in another container in the fridge to use in other recipes.

Snack

RAW VEGGIES & TARATOR A GOGO

Preparation time: 10 minutes | Servings: 2

A lighter option to veggies and hummus, especially when you are having it as a snack and not a meal. Tarator has almost the same ingredients as hummus, except the chickpeas.

And when you've got leftovers, you better make good use of them, and what is better than eating more veggies!

Ingredients

1 bunch of radishes
2 cucumbers, cut into sticks
¼ cup grape tomatoes
A handful of sweet peas
4 baby bell pepper
Handful of asparagus
½ ripe avocado

¼ cup leftover tarator from yesterday's dinner.

SAUTÉED DANDELION GREENS & BEET SALAD

Dandelion greens are so overlooked especially in the U.S. I personally consider them as the most powerful greens you can ever eat. As I mentioned before, your liver is the main organ of detoxification, and there are certain foods that your liver adores like beets, arugula, grapefruit and dandelions! Bitter foods help stimulate the liver to produce bile which emulsifies fats and renders nutrients which are crucial for digestion and absorption of fat-soluble vitamins. I was lucky enough to grow up eating this meal that my mom used to make because she considered it to be good at preventing anemia, and she wasn't wrong at all because dandelion greens are so rich in iron, especially when cooked. You may be probably asking if it is delicious, well, I can tell you that I always wished I could eat the whole thing and didn't have to share it with my siblings.

Preparation time: 15 minutes | Cooking time: 20 minutes
Total time: 35 minutes | Servings: 2

DANDELION GREENS

Ingredients

6 cups of water
2 bunches of dandelion greens, chopped (1 to 1½ inch thick) and rinsed
1 bunch of cilantro, rinsed, drained and minced
1 small onion, diced
4 cloves of garlic, finely minced
½ tsp. sea salt
2 lemons, juiced

Directions

1. In a big pot, on high heat, bring 6 cups of water to a boil.
2. Meanwhile, chop the dandelion greens, starting from the stems (1/2 inch length) and going up (1 inch to 1½ inch).
3. Wash and drain.
4. Add the chopped greens to the boiling water, bring to a boil again, then lower the heat to medium and let cook for 10 minutes or until stems are tender.
5. Drain using a colander and rinse with cold water until cooled down.
6. Squeeze with your hands to remove excess water and bitterness.
7. In a skillet, heat 1 tbsp avocado oil.
8. Add onions, garlic and sauté until the onions are golden brown.
9. Add minced cilantro with a pinch of sea salt and sauté for 1 minute.
10. Add the chopped dandelion greens with sea salt and let cook for 5 minutes.
11. Turn off the heat and add lemon juice and adjust salt to taste.

If you are not a fan of beets, this simple salad is going to change your mind. In Chinese medicine, beets are known to support the gallbladder which is considered responsible for passion, inspiration, action and assertiveness in our life, so if you are feeling uninspired, unmotivated or stuck maybe you should give your gallbladder some love by eating some of the food that supports its balance.

Those foods are beets, carrots, celery, radishes, dandelion, kale, garlic, basil, oranges, lemon, cayenne, all used in these recipes. Other things that support your gallbladder are:

- *Movement (exercise, dance, hiking, walking)*
- *Rest & sleep especially after 11 pm.*
- *Positive thinking*
- *Expressing your emotions and feelings freely*
- *Center yourself in love*

BEET SALAD

Ingredients

3 cooked beets, cut into cubes

Dressing ingredients
1 clove of garlic
1 lemon, juiced
1 tbsp. olive oil
Pinch of sea salt

Directions

1. Whisk the dressing ingredients together in a small bowl or jar.
2. Add the cooked beets to a medium-size bowl.
3. Add the dressing and mix.
4. Serve with sautéed dandelion.
5. Eat the whole salad. As for the sautéed dandelions, eat as much as you want.
6. You can keep leftovers sautéed dandelions in a sealed container or zip lock bag in the freezer for next week.

Day Four

SAVOR & NOURISH

Affirmation

Repeat with every meal.

- *I am nourishing my body with food from Mother Earth and my body thanks me.*

- *Even though my body knows what to do with any given food, it still appreciates my support.*

- *I love supporting my body in the best way I can.*

Breakfast
QUINOA MEGHLI (OR QUINOA PORRIDGE)

Preparation time: 5 minutes | Cooking time: 10 minutes
Total time: 15 minutes | Servings: 2

Meghli is a traditional Levantine pudding made with white rice flour, spices, water and sugar, topped with soaked nuts and raisins and offered to people as a celebration of a baby's birth. It was my favorite, especially with all those yummy toppings. I decided to recreate it in a healthier version, using only whole foods like quinoa instead of white rice flour and dates to replace white sugar.

I only used cinnamon in this recipe because I wanted to keep it simple and not overwhelm you with anise and caraway, but if you are familiar with them, do use them for sure. To my surprise, the results came out better than I imagined! Some people couldn't even tell it wasn't the original recipe!

You can eat this for breakfast or as a dessert and in both cases benefit from an array of nutrients especially if you are looking for a high protein breakfast recipe that doesn't include animal products. I hope you like it as much as I do. You can make this recipe the night before, so in the morning you will have breakfast ready as it tastes even better when chilled.

Ingredients

1 cup cooked quinoa
2 cups water
1 tsp. cinnamon powder

8 pitted medjool dates
Tiny pinch of sea salt

Toppings

1 tsp. unsweetened shredded coconut
Up to 1 tbsp. soaked almonds
Up to 1 tbsp. soaked pistachios

Up to 1 tbsp. soaked walnuts
Up to 1 tbsp. soaked pine nuts
1 tsp. raisins

Directions

1. Rinse the quinoa and drain.
2. Place in a medium pot with all the remaining ingredients.
3. Bring to a boil on high heat, uncovered.
4. Turn heat to low, cover the pot and let it simmer for 10 minutes.
5. With an immersion blender, blend the mixture until you get a smooth pudding consistency.
6. Pour into individual serving cups or bowls.
7. Let cool.
8. Garnish with shredded coconut, soaked nuts and raisins.
9. Keep in fridge until it is time to serve.

BLUEBERRY BOWL

Preparation time: 5 minutes | Servings: 1

When I was studying at IIN (Institute for Integrative Nutrition), I remember David Wolfe's lecture about raw food, so passionate about the miraculous power of nature's food. And at some point, he started talking about blueberries and how they support and maintain eye health, and how after eating blueberries for days, he experienced better eyesight! It was eye-opening for me how Mother Earth has everything we need to thrive and feel good. Yes, well-being is always available to us!

Ingredients

1 cup of fresh organic blueberries

Preferably choose organic whenever possible, especially those fruits and vegetables with thin skin like berries, apples, grapes, cherries, and leafy greens of course (all skin).

You can also refer to the ***dirty dozen/clean fifteen*** listen to check which produce to buy organic and which ones not to really stress about like avocados and watermelon for example.

Directions

1. Rinse the blueberries with fresh water.
2. Drain.
3. Serve and enjoy every blueberry with a grateful heart.
4. Feel the gratitude in your heart to be able to enjoy such an amazing and delicious fruit.
5. Enjoy!

Lunch
STUFFED PORTOBELLO PIZZAS

Not your grandma's pizza for sure but how nice it is to have substitutes and a break from all kinds of flours, breads, and pizza crusts? Another generous act of Nature that shapes some veggies in such a magical way! Portobellos are so versatile and perfectly shaped and textured, you can create anything with them: burgers, pizzas, "steak" and stuff them with anything!

Preparation time: 10 minutes | Cooking Time: 20 minutes
Total Time: 30 minutes | Servings: 3

Ingredients

For the portobello mushrooms
6 portobello mushrooms
½ cup grape tomatoes, cut in halves
6 Vegan cheese slices of choice
4 tbsp liquid aminos or tamari
2 tbsp avocado oil
¼ tsp. black pepper
¼ cup pitted sliced black olives
Fresh oregano leaves

For the refried beans
1 tbsp. avocado oil
1 cup cooked black beans
¼ tsp. cayenne pepper
¼ tsp. cumin powder

It is totally fine to use BPA-free canned beans or you can find the paper packaged ones.
Pinch of sea salt

Directions

To make the portobello pizzas:

1. Preheat oven at 350 Fahrenheit.
2. Rinse portobello mushrooms with water and drain.
3. Using a paper towel, tap to remove excess water.
4. Place the mushrooms on a baking sheet, facing up.
5. In a small bowl, whisk liquid aminos (or shoyu), avocado oil and black pepper.
6. Fill each portobello mushroom with approx. 1 tbsp of this mixture and let it sit for 5 minutes so it gets well absorbed.
7. Cover tray with foil paper and bake the mushrooms for 10 minutes.

Meanwhile, prepare the refried black beans

1. Preheat a skillet on medium heat with 1 tbsp. avocado oil.
2. Add the drained beans and stir frequently for 3 minutes.
3. Add salt, cumin and cayenne pepper and let simmer for 5 minutes on low heat.
4. Fill each mushroom with refried black beans, a slice of cheese, cherry tomatoes, olives and fresh oregano.
5. Remove foil and bake for another 10 minutes or until the cheese has melted.
6. Garnish with fresh oregano leaves and black pepper to taste.
7. Enjoy 2 portobello pizzas.
8. If not sharing with another person, freeze them in a sealed container for next week.

VILLAGER'S SNACK

Preparation time: 5 minutes | Servings: 1-2

This snack is inspired by the end of summer days in my village when a certain type of sour apples grow, I think they are called Bramley apples (teffeh mwachah). We take a plate with salt and a knife and pick the largest apple from the tree, sit under the tree and enjoy a fresh taste of sour salty and juicy goodness!

For this snack, I used Granny Smith apples for they are the closest to the apples from my village.

Ingredients

1 or 2 Granny Smith apples
Pinch of sea salt

Directions

1. Wash the apples.
2. Cut them into slices and sprinkle with a pinch of sea salt.
3. Enjoy.

Dinner

HUMMUS RICE CAKES

You're probably craving some sort of "bread" or "cracker" texture by now, so here is a treat for you since you made it to the 4th day of your detox. Make sure you choose brown rice cakes that are low in sodium if possible.

As you may have noticed, we are adding in all the high vibrational food during these 7 days so we can restore a positive relationship with whole foods and get used to the abundance of fruits and vegetables and ways of eating them. Getting familiar with new ways of eating will change our habits of easily reaching out to bread or crackers or chips as our main source of nourishment.

This does not mean we are going to rule out those foods forever, as there are great options out there, but it is good to give our body a break and love it up with vibrant colorful foods, at least during these 7 days! And I am sure that when you experience the effect this food has on you, you will feel inspired to give it to your body more often.

HUMMUS

Preparation time: 15 minutes | Servings: 4

Hummus has become universal now, everybody loves it! Not only because hummus is made with the healthiest combination of protein, carbs and fat but also because it is so filling and satisfying and so easy to make at home using simple ingredients. Being Lebanese, I know a thing or two about how hummus should taste and feel so you can trust me on this one!

Ingredients

2 cups cooked or canned chickpeas
1/3 cup freshly squeezed lemon juice (approx. 2 lemons)
¼ cup tahini
2 cloves of garlic + pinch of sea salt (makes ½ tbsp. garlic puree)
1 tsp. sea salt
¼ cup water (room temperature)
Pinch of cayenne pepper

Directions

1. You can use a blender or a food processor to make the Hummus.
2. First, crush the garlic with the pinch of salt using a pestle & mortar to release its juices and flavor.
3. Add the lemon juice, salt, cayenne pepper and garlic to the blender or food processor.
4. Blend until smooth.
5. Drain the chickpeas and add them to the blender with the tahini, and blend again, adding water little by little until desired consistency. (it depends on how well cooked the chickpeas are, if they are more or less soft, you can add up to 1/3 cup of water max to reach the desired consistency. (I usually add ¼ cup as in the recipe).

You are only going to need ½ cup hummus to make the rice cake hummus.

Preserve another ½ cup in a small bowl, covered with a thin layer of olive oil to use tomorrow as a side for the kale salad.

Keep leftovers in a sealed container in the freezer for next week so you can use it a dip for veggies or add it to your salads or sandwiches.

HUMMUS RICE CAKES

Ingredients

2 brown rice cakes
½ cup hummus
10 grape tomatoes, cut in halves
2 radishes, thinly sliced
1 cucumber, thinly sliced
Mint leaves for garnish
Cayenne pepper to taste

Directions

1. Spread ¼ cup of hummus on each rice cake.
2. Top with tomatoes, cucumbers, radishes, mint leaves and sprinkle cayenne pepper to taste.
3. Enjoy.

Day Five

ALLOW

Affirmation

Repeat with every meal.

- *I am whole and well.*
- *My body keeps getting better and better as the days go by, the more I allow it.*
- *My whole body constantly supports every part of my being, including my physical body.*

SCRAMBLED TOFU

Preparation time: 10 minutes | Cooking time: 20 minutes
Total time: 30 minutes | Servings: 4

I always make this recipe whenever I have friends over and want to impress them with some plant-based goodness. It works every single time! Some even thought it was scrambled eggs!

It's my kids and husband's favorite too, there is never enough leftovers, no matter if I double or triple the recipe!

This meal is so comforting and a great way to introduce the mighty turmeric into your diet in a delicious appealing way. I am assuming you all know about the amazing anti-inflammatory properties of turmeric which has been called the miracle spice.

Oh and make sure you use organic tofu where available, and the sprouted kind, for better digestion and health benefits.

Ingredients

2 tbsp. avocado oil

3 cloves of garlic, finely minced

1 leek, cut lengthwise then finely chopped
(½ inch thick)

2 cups of fresh sliced crimini mushrooms
(or white mushrooms)

1 ripe tomato, diced (approx. ½ cup)

1 extra firm tofu package (14 oz or 400 gr approx.)

2 tbsp. liquid aminos or tamari

1 tsp. turmeric + ½ tsp black pepper

Pinch of sea salt

1 tbsp. nutritional yeast
(optional but highly recommended)

1 big tomato to use as "bread"
(optional)

Directions

1. First, remove the tofu from the package, drain and wrap it in paper towel to remove excess water.
2. Heat the oil briefly on medium heat in a big skillet.
3. Add garlic & leeks and sauté for 2 minutes, stirring frequently.
4. Add mushrooms and sauté for 3 minutes or until golden brown.
5. Unwrap the tofu and crumble it over the skillet using both hands.
6. Add tomatoes and stir well with the garlic, mushroom, leek mixture.
7. Add turmeric, black pepper and shoyu and mix again.
8. Add nutritional yeast, if using any and stir.
9. Let the mixture simmer on low heat for 10 minutes, or until excess liquid has evaporated, stirring from time to time.

Adjust seasoning to taste and serve in a plate with greens, olives and radishes.

Serving suggestion (as pictured): Serve on a large tomato slice that would serve as "bread" so you can eat it with your hand or using a fork and a knife.

LEMON WITH SEA SALT

Preparation time: 5 minutes | Servings: 1

I know, not your regular snack, but it's one of my mom's and my favorites. I grew up eating it a lot! And do not worry, my teeth are just fine but hey, don't overdo it!

This simple snack helps your digestion after a heavy meal, will keep your breath fresh, provide you with Vitamin C, give you energy and soothe a sore throat.

Did you know lemons and salt are known in many cultures to steer away from any negative energy?

Another unusual use of lemon that I swear by is using lemon as a natural deodorant! Just don't eat it afterwards!

Ingredients

1 lemon
Pinch of sea salt

Directions

1. Wash the lemon and peel it.
2. Slice it and sprinkle it with sea salt.
3. Enjoy!

Note: If you do not like lemons, you can use grapefruit instead.

Lunch
MEDITERRANEAN KALE SALAD & LEFTOVER HUMMUS

There is nothing in the food kingdom that you cannot transform into a delicious and pleasurable thing to eat, including kale, which is widely celebrated as a superfood, but sometimes disliked and avoided for its unwieldy nature. The secret in this recipe lies in the dressing and the massage you are going to give to your beloved kale!

Preparation time: 15 minutes | Total Time: 15 minutes | Servings: 1

Ingredients

1 bunch of dino kale, stems removed (soaked in water with 2 tbsp of vinegar for 5 minutes)
¼ cup pomegranate seeds
1 tsp. sesame seeds

Dressing
¼ cup fresh lemon juice (3 lemons approx.)
1 tbsp. tahini paste
½ ripe avocado (small to medium)
¼ tsp. sea salt
Pinch of black pepper

Directions

1. To clean the kale, soak them in water + 2 tbsp vinegar for 5 minutes.
2. Rinse well and let drain well on paper towels.
3. Meanwhile prepare the dressing by blending all the dressing ingredients in a blender until smooth and creamy.
4. Adjust consistency by adding 1 to 2 tbsp water.
5. Chop kale leaves roughly.
6. Add to a big salad bowl.
7. Pour the dressing over kale and massage it thoroughly until the kale looks and feel softer to the touch.
8. This way you are making your raw kale more digestible and flavorful.
9. Serve with pomegranate seeds and a sprinkle of sesame seeds.
10. Enjoy with ½ cup hummus leftovers on the side.

Snack

WATERMELON PIZZA

Preparation time: 5 minutes | Servings: 1

This recipe is about tapping into your creativity when making food, widening your horizons and experimenting with new concepts.

Staying open and adopting a beginner's mind is crucial when you want to create change and transformation.

Again, not your regular pizza, but a fun and creative way to do it and give birth to new healthy snacks that are appealing to both kids and adults.

Ingredients

1 round slice of watermelon
¼ cup macadamia parmesan* (see recipe below)
5 olives, sliced
Fresh basil leaves

MACADAMIA PARMESAN

Ingredients

1 cup raw macadamia nuts
½ tsp. garlic powder
1 tbsp. nutritional yeast
1/8 tsp. black pepper
¼ tsp. sea salt

Directions

1. Pulse macadamia nuts in a food processor until finely crumbly.
2. Make sure not to over-process and create nut butter. Just enough time to create parmesan texture.
3. Add the rest of the ingredients and give it a brief pulse/mix.
4. Preserve in a jar in the fridge and feel free to sprinkle over your salads, pastas, bowls, and other dishes.

To make the pizza

1. Cut a round watermelon slice, 1 inch thick.
2. Sprinkle 2 tbsp parmesan cheese evenly.
3. Top with olives slices and fresh basil leaves.
4. Slice and enjoy the whole pizza.

RED LENTIL SOUP

Comfort food is great nutrition at its best. So simple to make and so filling you wouldn't need any other food to pair with it. This recipe is perfect to make on days when you literally have only 7 minutes to prepare something that is nourishing and filling for yourself and your family. The other 43 minutes, you do not have to be in the kitchen, just make sure to set the timer.

Lentils are rich in fiber and iron and are high in most types of vitamin B and folate. According to the Harvard School of Public Health, a cooked cup of lentils provides 18 g of protein!

I am not a nutritionist or dietician, and to be honest, I believe all Mother Earth food is extremely and uniquely nutritious, so I personally do not focus a lot on researching the different types of minerals or vitamins that each food contains, but I know some of you do, and this is why you see me sharing this kind of information from time to time.

Preparation time: 7 minutes | Cooking time: 43 minutes
Total time: 50 minutes | Servings: 2-3

Ingredients

1 ½ cups red lentils
4 ½ cups water
1 onion, cut in half-moon slices (approx. 1 cup)

1 tsp. sea salt
1 tsp. cumin powder

Directions

1. In a big bowl, rinse the lentils with fresh water until the water is almost clear.
2. Drain and set aside.
3. Cut the onion in half-moon slices and place in a big pot with the drained lentils on top.
4. Add water and cumin powder.
5. Bring to boil on high heat, pot uncovered.
6. Lower heat, cover the pot and let simmer for 30 minutes.
7. Add salt and blend using an immersion blender until smooth and creamy.
8. Bring to a boil again on high heat.
9. Let simmer for another 10 minutes with the pot uncovered, on low heat, stirring from time to time.

Serve up to 2 cups and garnish with fresh cilantro leaves, arugula, olives and radishes. Freeze any leftover in a sealed container to use in the next coming weeks.
Note: If you do not have an immersion blender, you will have to transfer the mixture to a regular blender and blend until smooth and creamy. Just make you let it cool down a little bit before adding it to the blender to avoid any damage to the container.

Day Six

COMMITT

Affirmation

Repeat with every meal.

- *Thank you, beloved body, I love you, you are amazing.*

- *I know I haven't always been good to you, sometimes bashing you, talking badly to you and comparing you to others but today I've decided to change my relationship with you to a loving and supportive one. Even if I don't really feel like telling you I love you 100%, I am still going to say it until I mean it.*

- *I love you.*

Breakfast
CELERY & APPLE JUICE

Preparation time: 5 minutes | Servings: 1

I am sure many of you heard about the new superstar CELERY and many of you joined the celery juice challenge initiated by the medical medium Anthony Williams.

I tried it myself for 2 weeks on an empty stomach, it was a great experience, I felt more energetic and vibrant for sure.

But if you are expecting to change your life from food alone, it won't happen..

Many years ago, I thought if I changed my food, my life would be perfect! That was before I discovered that change starts from within and that food, while important, is only a part of the equation.

So bottom line, celery is great, as well as all fruits, vegetables and all Mother Nature's source of nourishment, let us appreciate them and feel grateful to live in such abundance without obsession or rigidity.

Ingredients

1 bunch celery
1 Granny Smith apple

Directions

1. Rinse the celery thoroughly with water, then soak for 5 minutes in a big bowl of water and a tbsp of apple cider vinegar.
2. Run celery sticks and the apples through your juicer and drink immediately.
3. If you do not have a juicer, chop the celery sticks and add to a high-speed blender with the apples and a splash of water until smooth.
4. Strain to remove the pulp and drink on an empty stomach.

GOING NUTS

Preparation time: 5 minutes | Servings: 1

Ingredients

1 tbsp. soaked almonds
1 tbsp. soaked pistachios
1 tbsp. soaked walnuts
1 tbsp. soaked pine nuts
2 tbsp. pomegranate seeds
Pinch of nutmeg
1 tsp. maple syrup
½ tsp. orange blossom water (or rose water)
½ tsp. lemon juice

Directions

1. Add soaked nuts & pomegranate seeds to a small bowl and mix.
2. Whisk the dressing ingredients together and pour over your snack.
3. Enjoy!

Lunch
VEGAN TUNA BUDDHA BOWL

Preparation time: 25 minutes | Servings: 1

Ingredients

1 cup chickpea tuna
1 cup mixed greens of choice
1 avocado, split into 2 halves
½ endive
1 carrot, finely grated
6 grape tomatoes, cut in halves
1 cucumber, shaved in ribbons
Handful of sprouts of choice
2 tbsp. pitted olives
3 baby bell peppers (or ½ big one, chopped)
3 radishes, sliced
1 tbsp. pumpkin seeds

Dressing

2 tbsp. apple cider vinegar
1 tbsp. lemon juice
White part of 1 scallion, finely chopped
2 tbsp. minced parsley
2 tbsp. liquid aminos or shoyu
2 tbsp. olive oil

To assemble your buddha bowl

1. Use a big salad bowl.
2. Start with the greens.
3. Arrange the rest of the ingredients as shown or to taste.
4. I filled the avocados with chickpea tuna as a fun way to serve this buddha bowl.
5. Add the dressing and enjoy.

TO MAKE THE "TUNA"

Preparation time: 10 minutes | Servings: 2

Ingredients

1 can chickpea (2 cups)
2 tbsp. lemon juice
2 tbsp. tahini (or vegan mayo)
1 tbsp. liquid aminos or tamari
1 stalk of green onions, finely chopped (approx. 2 tbsp)
1 tsp. dulse seaweed (optional but recommended: if unavailable, use nori flakes instead)
Cayenne pepper to taste

Directions

1. In a shallow bowl, using a fork, or a potato masher, mash the chickpeas to mimic tuna texture.
2. Add the rest of the ingredients and mix until well incorporated.
3. Set aside.
4. Store leftovers in freezer in a sealed container.

Snack

CAROB SMOOTHIE PICK-ME-UP

Preparation time: 5 minutes | Servings: 1

Ingredients

½ cup water
6 pitted medjool dates
½ small avocado
½ cup frozen blueberries
2 tbsp. carob powder

Directions

1. Add all the ingredients to a high-speed blender and blend until smooth.
2. Serve and top with some berries and cacao nibs. Enjoy.

HEMP TABBOULI

Preparation time: 20 minutes | Total time: 20 minutes | Servings: 1

TO MAKE THE TABBOULI

Ingredients

1 bunch of parsley, finely minced (approx. 2 cups minced parsley)
1 big tomato, small diced (approx. 1 cup diced tomato)
2 tbsp. finely minced yellow onion + 1/8 tsp allspice + pinch sea salt + pinch cinnamon
¼ tsp. allspice
Pinch of cinnamon
Pinch of black pepper
2 tbsp. hemp seeds

For the dressing
1 lemon, juiced (approx. 3 tbsp)
2 tbsp. olive oil
¼ tsp. sea salt
1 romaine lettuce heart to serve with

Directions

1.   First, rinse all the ingredients with fresh water and drain in a big colander.
2.   Spread the parsley on paper towel to remove excess moisture.
3.   Note: I prefer to wash the parsley ahead of time so it has time to dry before I mince, this will keep the parsley from wilting.
4.   Start with the onion, cut 1 small onion in quarters and using one quarter, finely mince it.
5.   Add a pinch of salt, allspice and cinnamon and give it another chop to kind of mix the onions with the salt and spices. Transfer to a bowl.
6.   Shop the parsley really fine and transfer to the bowl.
7.   Dice the tomatoes and transfer to the bowl.
8.   Prepare the dressing by whisking all ingredients in a small bowl and pour them onto the salad ingredients.
9.   Mix thoroughly with the remaining salt and spices.
10. Add hemp seeds and give it another mix.
11. Serve with lettuce.
12. Enjoy the whole salad.

NOTE: Soak 1 cup of raw cashews to make the cashew cheese on day 7.

Day Seven

MANIFEST

Affirmation

Repeat with every meal.

- Close your eyes, picture the ideal image of the body you wish you have.
- See yourself in that body, walking, dancing, going to work, going out, sleeping, and eating.
- Give thanks as if it already happened.
- Know that the manifestation of it will be before your eyes soon.
- I love all expressions of my body and I know they depend on the way
- I am feeling on the inside most of the time.
- Today I am feeling beautiful, healthy, sexy, radiant, glowing, thriving, ecstatic and full of hope. And so it is.

BEAUTY & GLOW SMOOTHIE

Preparation time: 10 minutes | Servings: 2

Ingredients

½ cup water (you can use 8 ice cubes instead)
2 frozen ripe bananas chunks (approx. 1 ½ cups)
1 cup frozen blueberries
1 peeled cucumber (¼ cup cucumber slices)
1 cup pineapple chunks (you can use frozen)
1 tbsp aloe vera (that you scoop out of aloe vera leaf) (optional)
1 tsp. lemon juice
½ medium avocado
½ small raw beet

Directions

1. Add the ingredients to the blender, starting with the water. Blend until smooth.
2. Serve in a bowl and top with fresh blueberries, cacao nibs and edible flowers.
3. Enjoy.

Add leftovers to popsicle molds and freeze them. Makes a great snack!

Snack
ROASTED PUMPKIN SEED SHELLS

Preparation time: 5 minutes | Servings: 1

This snack is so filling you won't feel hungry until lunchtime.

That's because pumpkin seed shells are so high in protein, can you believe ¼ cup has 9 g?

You can get unsalted pumpkin seed shells or lightly salted which of course are more delicious.

Lunch
FISH TOFU WITH ARUGULA SALAD

Preparation time: 25 minutes | *Servings: 1*

Ingredients

1 package of extra-firm tofu (12 or 14 oz, approx. 400 gr.)
2 tbsp. Old Bay Spice (or just use fish spices if you can't find Old Bay spices)
2 tbsp. liquid aminos (or tamari)
1 tsp. nutritional yeast
1 tbsp. coconut oil

To make the salad
3 cups baby arugula (or your favorite greens)
1 avocado
1 cup grape tomatoes
1 watermelon radish, thinly sliced
1 cucumber thinly sliced and rolled into ribbons
1 tbsp. hemp hearts

To make the salad dressing
1 lemon, juiced
1 tsp. olive oil
1 tsp. dijon mustard
1 tsp. liquid aminos (or tamari)
Pinch of black pepper

Directions

1. Remove the tofu from its packaging, drain and wrap with a paper towel.
2. Cut the tofu in 7 rectangles, then cut each rectangle diagonally in 2 triangles.
3. You should have 14 triangles in total.
4. Place tofu slices on a baking sheet & season with Old Bay Spice.
5. Use 1 tsp to sprinkle over each side, making sure all the tofu slices are well coated with the spices.
6. Heat the coconut oil in a large non-stick skillet on medium to high flame until shimmering.
7. Transfer tofu slices to the skillet and place them in a single layer.
8. Pan fry on each side for 4 to 5 minutes on medium to high flame.
9. Tofu should be golden brown.
10. Add 2 tbsp. liquid aminos over the tofu and let sizzle for a minute, then sprinkle 1 tsp of nutritional yeast and let cook for another 4 minutes or until desired crispiness.
11. Transfer the browned crispy tofu to a cooling rack while you assemble your salad.
12. Assemble salad by adding all the salad ingredients
13. Whisk all your dressing ingredients in a small bowl and drizzle on top of salad.
14. Serve in a plate with some fish tofu.

Note: The tofu should be consumed no longer than an hour after cooking otherwise it will start losing its crispiness.

Dinner

CASHEW CHEESE SPREAD ON HEMP TOAST

Preparation time: 20 minutes | *Total time: 20 minutes* | *Servings: 1*

HEMP BREAD

Ingredients

½ cup zucchini cubes (approx. half a medium-size zucchini)
½ cup water
2 tsp. lemon juice
½ tsp. sea salt
1 cup hemp hearts
2 tbsp. sesame seeds
1 tbsp. zaatar mix
½ cup oat flour
1 tbsp. flax meal

Directions

1. Preheat oven at 275 Fahrenheit.
2. Line a baking tray with silicone sheet and set aside.
3. Using a high-speed blender, blend zucchini, water, lemon juice and salt until super smooth.
4. Transfer to a bowl.
5. Add hemp hearts, sesame seeds, zaatar and oat flour and mix with a spoon.
6. Add flax meal and mix again until well incorporated.
7. Spread the mixture on the silicone sheet, using a flat spatula to form a ¼ inch thick rectangle.
8. Using a knife, define the bread slices size to taste.
9. Bake at 275 F for 30 minutes.
10. Turn off oven and let the bread rest in the oven for 10 to 20 minutes to make sure the toasted bread is completely dry.
11. Separate the bread slices with your hands.
12. Let them cool.
13. You can store them in a ziplock bag at room temperature for the first 2 days, then in the fridge up to 4 days. Or freeze up to 4 months.

CASHEW CHEESE

Ingredients

1 cup soaked cashews (soaked overnight)
2 tbsp. nutritional yeast
1 garlic clove
2 tbsp. lemon juice
¼ tsp. salt or more to taste
½ tsp. red pepper flakes (if you don't like it spicy, omit this)
1/8 tsp. paprika
2 tbsp. water
3 basil leaves
½ tsp. maple syrup

Directions

1. Using a high-speed blender, add all the ingredients starting with the lemon juice and blend until smooth and creamy.
2. You may need to turn off the blender to scrape down the sides and proceed again a couple of times.
3. Transfer to a bowl.

TO MAKE THE CHEESE TOASTS

Ingredients

2 hemp breads
¼ cup cashew cheese spread
¼ cup cherry tomatoes cut in quarters each
Basil leaves
Edible flowers

Directions

1. Spread 2 tbsp of cashew cream cheese on each hemp bread slice, using a small knife.
2. Top with grape tomatoes and fresh basil leaves.
3. Use edible flowers if you'd like.
4. Enjoy.

OR GRILLED VEGETABLES WITH CASHEW CHEESE

Ingredients

1 bunch asparagus
1 bunch of carrots
1 head cauliflower
¼ cup avocado oil
½ tsp. sea salt
½ tsp. black pepper

Directions

1. Preheat oven to 375F.
2. Rinse all vegetables and pat dry with a paper towel.
3. You need 2 baking trays lined with silicone sheets or parchment paper.
4. Spread the carrots and asparagus, making sure they are not overlapping, on the first baking sheet.
5. Cut the cauliflower into florets and spread in the second baking tray.
6. Drizzle avocado oil, salt and pepper evenly on top of the veggies. Using your hands, make sure they are well coated with oil.
7. Bake for 15 to 20 minutes:
8. You can broil for 2 minutes to give them that broiled look.
9. Serve grilled vegetables with ¼ cup of cashew chipotle cheese. Enjoy.

Bonus Recipe

GODDESS CAROB CAKE

I made this cake for Evana's 6th birthday and I would love to share it with you as a celebration of your awakened goddess birthday.

Send an email to *nathalie.sader@gmail.com* asking to send you this recipe and celebrate with you!

REQUEST
RECIPE

Affirmations

For your easy reference, here's the original text for affirmations.

Day One

SET THE INTENTION

AFFIRMATION
Repeat with every meal.

Look at your food and give thanks.

Close your eyes, place your hand on your heart, connect to the love within you.

Take 5 deep breaths as follows: Take a deep breath, counting to 5 for the inhale, hold your breath, count to 3, and exhale, counting to 7.

Place the palm of your hand on above your food and say this affirmation out loud 5 times: I set the intention for this food to deeply nourish and support my body.

Notice how you feel. Smile. Eat with enjoyment.

Day Two

TRUST

AFFIRMATION
Repeat for every meal.

I relax and enjoy my food knowing that my body is an expert at transforming this food into fuel, energy and nourishment.

I fully trust my body.

Relaxing allows my body to do its job without resistance and stress.

Day Three

APPRECIATE

AFFIRMATION
Repeat for every meal.

I fully love and accept my body. I am so grateful for all the things my body does for me without my intervention: breathing, my heart beating, cell regeneration, digestion and more.

I let my body do its job with ease and grace.

Day Four

SAVOR & NOURISH

AFFIRMATION
Repeat for every meal.

I am nourishing my body with food from Mother Earth and my body thanks me.

Even though my body knows what to do with any given food, it still appreciates my support.

I love supporting my body in the best way I can.

ALLOW

AFFIRMATION
Repeat for every meal.

I am whole and well.

My body keeps getting better and better as the days go by, the more I allow it.

My whole body constantly supports every part of my being, including my physical body.

COMMITT

AFFIRMATION
Repeat for every meal.

Thank you, beloved body, I love you, you are amazing.

I know I haven't always been good to you, sometimes bashing you, talking badly to you and comparing you to others but today I've decided to change my relationship with you to a loving and supportive one. Even if I don't really feel like telling you I love you 100%, I am still going to say it until I mean it.

I love you.

MANIFEST

AFFIRMATION
Repeat for every meal.

Close your eyes, picture the ideal image of the body you wish you have.

See yourself in that body, walking, dancing, going to work, going out, sleeping, and eating.

Give thanks as if it already happened.

Know that the manifestation of it will be before your eyes soon.

I love all expressions of my body and I know they depend on the way I am feeling on the inside most of the time.

Today I am feeling beautiful, healthy, sexy, radiant, glowing, thriving, ecstatic and full of hope.

And so it is.

List of Ingredients

Fresh Vegetables

Kale	Baby arugula
Avocados	Radishes
Lemons	Sweet peas
Carrots	Bell pepper
Yellow onions	Asparagus
Cabbage	Dandelions greens
Tomatoes	Portobello mushrooms
Sweet potato	Leek
Lime	Celery
Mushrooms	Mixed greens
Marinated baby artichokes	Endives
Beets	Scallions
Cherry tomatoes	Romaine lettuce
Butter lettuce	Watermelon radish
Grape tomatoes	Zucchini
Cucumber	Cauliflower

Fresh Fruits

Bananas

Strawberries

Granny smith apples

Raspberries

Pomegranate

Blood orange

Watermelon

Blueberries

Pineapple

Frozen Fruits

Frozen bananas

Frozen blueberries

Frozen pineapples

Dried Fruits

Medjool dates

Raisins

Shredded coconut

Beans and Legumes

(Dry or Canned BPA-free lining)

Lentils Brown dry

Red Lentils dry

Kidney beans canned

Chickpeas canned

Black beans canned

Tofu organic

Nuts and Nut Butter

Almonds raw

Pistachios raw

Pine nuts raw

Macadamia raw

Cashews raw

Almond butter

Whole Grains

Quinoa

Corn kernels organic

Rolled oats regular

Non Dairy Milk and Yogurt

Almond milk unsweetened

Coconut milk unsweetened

Almond or coconut yogurt unsweetened

Seeds

Chia seeds*

Flaxmeal (ground flax seeds)*

Hemp seeds hearts*

Pumpkin seeds

Sesame seeds
See specialty ingredients

Natural Sweeteners

Maple syrup

Brown rice syrup*

Raw honey*

Coconut nectar*

Stevia*
Found at health food stores or online.

Condiments

Lemon juice

Sea salt

Cumin powder

Black pepper

Garlic fresh

Mint dried

Cayenne pepper

Red pepper flakes

Cinnamon powder

Liquid aminos*

Olives

Turmeric

Garlic powder

Nutmeg powder

Apple cider vinegar

Vegan mayonnaise
(optional, with tahini as alternative)

Allspice

Old bay spice

Dijon mustard

Fresh Herbs

Basil

Cilantro

Mint

Oregano

Parsley

Oils

Avocado oil

Coconut oil

Olive oil

Pasta, Flours and Breads

Brown rice tagliatelle or any gluten-free

pasta of choice

Oat flour

Brown rice cakes

Specialty Ingredients

You can find the following ingredients at most health food stores and some regular stores. If not available locally, order online from Amazon or another outlet.

HEMP HEARTS OR HEMP SEEDS

A superfood and "perfect protein," seeds of the hemp plant will not get you high. Rich in omega 3 and 6, high in fiber, they contain all 20 amino acids, including the 9 amino acids that our body cannot produce.

CACAO NIBS

Cacao nibs are crushed pieces of cacao beans derived from the cacao tree. Bitter in taste and rich in protein, fiber, good fats and minerals including magnesium, iron & zinc.

CHIA SEEDS

High-protein, omega-3 packed superfood, these tiny seeds, native of Mexico and Guatemala, are produced by a flowery plant in the mint family and cultivated in North and South America.

Very rich in fiber, manganese and calcium, chia seeds are a powerhouse of antioxidants. When soaked in water or liquids, they swell and become gelatinous which makes them great for puddings and an excellent egg replacement for baking.

ORANGE BLOSSOM WATER & ROSE WATER

A staple in Middle Eastern cuisine, these flower-scented and flavored waters elevate and satisfy your senses in the most beautiful way. In Lebanon, we use them in desserts, as a face wash, for irritated eyes, among other uses.

I like to make "white coffee" by boiling water, adding 1 tbsp of orange blossom water and a natural sweetener as a good digestive aid that is calming and delicious. You can find it in Middle Eastern stores in your area or at health food stores usually in the sweeteners aisle, or order online.

TAHINI

Staple of Middle Eastern cuisine, tahini is made from toasted sesame seeds that are grounded and hulled to produce the tahini paste. It is the main ingredient in hummus and is also used in desserts and to make dressings and sauces. High in healthy fats and amino acids, tahini is also rich in A, B & E vitamins, and minerals such as magnesium, iron and zinc. Available in health food stores, local groceries, and online.

LIQUID AMINOS

Gluten-free soy sauce alternative, usually made from soybeans treated with an acidic solution that breaks them down into free amino acids (building blocks of proteins). My favorite brand is Braggs liquid aminos. Tamari is also a gluten alternative to soy sauce, made from fermented soybeans usually free from additives. You can also get "coconut aminos" if you prefer to go soy-free, made by fermenting coconut sap.

Available in health and regular food stores Japanese and Chinese stores, and online.

VEGAN CHEESE SLICES

Vegan cheese slices are available in most food stores. There are many different brands but Dayia is my favorite. While it is not a whole food, you will only use it in one recipe, so consider it a treat.

TOFU

Tofu is a great source of protein and is very filling. Made from the curds of soy milk in a similar way that cheese is produced from cow's milk. Make sure to opt for organic tofu to avoid genetically modified tofu.

NUTRITIONAL YEAST

This flavorful condiment rich in B vitamins, especially B12, has a nutty cheesy & creamy taste and is usually used to make plant-based cheeses and sauces. An inactive type of yeast, it is made by culturing a yeast in a growth medium nutrient, usually sugar cane and beet molasses. The yeast is then deactivated with heat, washed, dried and ready to use.

SUNFLOWER SPROUTS

A good source of protein and vitamin C, made from sprouting (germinating) sunflower seeds. You can use any kinds of sprouts you like in the corresponding recipe: bean sprouts, nut sprouts, seed sprouts or grain sprouts. Sprouts ease digestion and help absorb nutrients.

DULSE FLAKES OR NORI FLAKES

Dried seaweeds provide fiber, protein, and are rich in trace minerals, vitamins, healthy fatty acids and antioxidants.

CAROB POWDER

Caffeine-free substitute for cacao powder, with a rich chocolate taste that is naturally sweet. Carob powder is made from carob pods' pulp that is dried, roasted and then ground into powder.
Just like cacao, carob comes from a tree. Carob is a good source of fiber, calcium and potassium.

ALOE VERA GEL

Made from the gel inside the aloe vera leaf. You can get it either by having the actual plant, opening a leaf and scooping out the gel with a spoon or by buying the aloe vera in a bottle from the health food store.

Aloe vera gel is a powerhouse of nutrients like no other including antioxidant vitamins like vitamins A, C, E, B12, folic acid and choline. Rich in minerals like calcium, potassium, magnesium, copper, zinc, it is also high in enzymes that help break down sugars and fats.
Aloe vera is known as a remedy for skin conditions. I personally use it for burns, sunburns and cuts.

Aloe vera is also great for constipation, just make sure to ask your health care provider in this case and use with moderation.

ZAATAR MIX

Another staple of Middle Eastern cuisine, this mix of dried thyme, sesame seeds and sumac will make any dish super flavorful. Found in Middle Eastern stores or in the spice section of grocery or health food stores.

EDIBLE FLOWERS

My favorites are pansies, violets, nasturtiums, roses and lemon blossoms, used in various dishes. Available in pots from a health food store but make sure they have not been sprayed or grow them yourself. You can also buy them in boxes in health food stores in the refrigerated herb section.

Ingredients Substitutes

Kale	Collard greens or spinach.
Hemp seeds	Chia seeds
Maple syrup	Brown rice syrup, date syrup, coconut nectar, raw honey
Sea salt	Himalayan salt
Rosewater and orange blossom water	Vanilla extract
Avocado oil	Grape seed oil for cooking, olive oil for salads
Kidney beans	Pinto beans, white beans
Liquid aminos	Tamari, coconut aminos or organic low sodium soy sauce
Baby arugula	Other greens
Dandelion greens	Collard greens
Tofu	Egg whites if you eat eggs
Leek	White onion
Macadamia	Almonds
Endive	Romaine lettuce heart, bok choy
Dulse flakes	Nori flakes
Watermelon radish	Red radish
Zaatar	Sumac
Carob powder	Raw cacao powder *(but you have to add sweet ingredients)*
Edible flowers	Fresh herbs
Aloe vera gel	Aloe vera juice
Almond yogurt	Coconut yogurt or organic soy yogurt
Almond milk	Can be replaced by coconut milk, rice milk, cashew milk or organic soy milk.

Shopping List

Produce

	DAY 1	DAY 2	DAY 3	DAY 4	DAY 5	DAY 6	DAY 7	TOTAL
Aloe vera (optional)							1 tbsp.	1 tbsp.
Baby Arugula			1 C				3 C	4 PC
Asparagus			Handful				1 bunch	1 bunch +
Avocado	1 & ½ PC	2 PC	1 & ½ PC		½ PC	1 & ½ PC	1 & ½ PC	8 & ½ PC
Bananas (frozen)	2 PC or 1½ C						2 PC or 1½ C	4 PC
Baby artichokes, marinated	6 PC							6 PC
Basil leaves		¼ C	10 to 20 leaves		8		3 +	1 bunch
Beetroot		4 PC	3 PC				½ PC	7 & ½ PC
Bell pepper, baby			4 PC			3 PC		7 PC
Blood orange			1 PC					1 PC
Blueberries				1 C				1 C
Blueberries, frozen						½ C	1 C	1 & ½ C
Butter lettuce		1 PC						1 PC
Cabbage head, small	1 PC							1 PC
Carrots	2 PC					1 PC	1 bunch	1 bunch +3PC
Cauliflower, small							1 PC	1 PC
Celery						1 bunch		1 bunch
Cherry tomatoes		1 C	½ C				¼ C	1 & ¾ C
Cilantro, bunch			1					1
Corn kernels		1 C						1 C
Cucumber			3 PC			1 PC	2 PC	6 PC

	DAY 1	DAY 2	DAY 3	DAY 4	DAY 5	DAY 6	DAY 7	TOTAL
Dandelion greens (bunch)			2					2
Endive						½ PC		½ PC
Flowers (edible of choice, opt.)							garnish	garnish
Garlic (cloves)	2	4	5	2	3		1	17
Garnett sweet potato (big)	1 PC							1 PC
Granny smith apple	1 PC			2 PC		1 PC		4 PC
Grape tomatoes			¼ C	1 C		6 PC	1 C	2½ C + 6PC
Greens (mixed of choice)						1 C		1 C
Kale (dino kale preferably)	2 leaves				1 bunch			1 bunch +2 leaves
Leek (bunch)					1			1
Lemons	4 PC	3 PC	4 PC	2 PC	4 PC	2 PC	2 PC	21 PC
Lettuce (romaine)						1 PC		
Lime	½ PC							½ PC
Mint leaves	Garnish			6				6 +
Mushrooms (fresh)	1 C or 4 oz	1 C			2 C			4 C
Onion (yellow)	1 PC		1 PC		1 PC	2 tbsp.		3 PC +2 tbsp.
Oregano (fresh)				Handful				Handful
Parsley (bunch)						1 bunch or 2 cups minced		1 bunch + 2 tbsp.
Pineapple (chunks)							1 C	1 C
Pomegranate seeds		2 tbsp.			¼ C	2 tbsp.		¼ C + 4 tbsp.
Portobello mushrooms				6 PC				6 PC
Pumpkin shells (roasted unsalted)							¼ C	¼ C
Radish (bunch)			1 bunch	2 PC		3 PC		1 bunch + 5 PC
Raspberries		¾ C						¾ C
Scallions						2 PC		2 PC
Sprouts of choice						Handful		Handful
Strawberries	½ C							½ C
Sweet peas			Handful					Handful
Tomato (big & ripe)	1 PC				2 PC	1 PC		4 PC
Watermelon (small)			½ PC		1 round slice			½ PC + 1 slice
Watermelon radishes							1	1 PC
Zucchini (cubed)							½ C	½ C

Non Dairy

	DAY 1	DAY 2	DAY 3	DAY 4	DAY 5	DAY 6	DAY 7	TOTAL
Almond milk *(unsweetened)*	1 C	1 C						2 C
Cheese, vegan, slices				6				6
Tofu, extra firm *(12 oz. package)*					1		1	2
Yogurt *(Unsweetened plant-based)*		½ C						½ C

Spices and Flavoring

	DAY 1	DAY 2	DAY 3	DAY 4	DAY 5	DAY 6	DAY 7	TOTAL
Allspice						½ tsp ~		½ tsp +
Apple cider vinegar						1 tbsp.		1 tbsp.
Black pepper	pinch		1/8 tsp.	¼ tsp.	1 tsp.	Pinch	Pinch + ½ tsp.	2 tsp. +
Cayenne pepper	pinch	To taste		¼ tsp +		To taste		~ ½ tsp.
Cinnamon		pinch	pinch	1 tsp.		Pinch		1 tsp. +
Cumin	½ tsp.	pinch		¼ tsp.	1 tsp.			~ 2 tsp.
Dijon mustard							1 tsp.	1 tsp.
Garlic powder					½ tsp.			½ tsp.
Liquid aminos		1 tbsp.	1 tbsp.	4 tbsp.	2 tbsp.	3 tbsp.	2 tbsp. + 1 tsp	15 tbsp. + 1 tsp.
Nutmeg						Pinch		Pinch
Nutritional yeast					2 tbsp.		1 tsp. + 2 tbsp.	4 tbsp. + 1 tsp.
Old Bay spice or fish spice							2 tbsp.	2 tbsp.
Paprika							1/8 tsp.	1/8 tsp.
Red pepper flakes	pinch						½ tsp.	Pinch + ½ tsp.
Sea salt	1 tsp. & ½	1 tsp & ½	¾ tsp.	1 tsp & 1/8	1 tsp. & ¾	¼ tsp.	1 tsp & ¼	2 tbsp.+ 2 tsp & 1/8 tsp
Turmeric					1 tsp.			1 tsp.

Dry Goods

	PREP	DAY 1	DAY 2	DAY 3	DAY 4	DAY 5	DAY 6	DAY 7	TOTAL
Almonds *(raw)*	1 C								1 C
Almond butter				1 tbsp.					1 tbsp.
Avocado oil		3 tsp.	2 tbsp.		3 tbsp.	2 tbsp.		¼ C	10 tbsp. + ¼ C
Black beans *(cooked)*					1 C				1 C
Brown rice cakes					2 PC				2 PC
Cacao nibs		1 tsp.		1 tsp.					2 tsp.
Carob powder							2 tbsp.		2 tbsp.
Cashews *(raw to soak for day 7)*							1 C		1 C
Chia seeds			¼ C						¼ C
Chickpea *(cooked)*			½ C	2 C			2 C		4 & ½ C
Coconut oil								1 tbsp.	1 tbsp.
Coconut *(shredded, unsweetened)*			1b tbsp.	1 tbsp.	1 tbsp.				3 tbsp.
Dates *(medjool)*			3 PC	8 PC	8 PC		6 PC		25 PC
Dulse seaweed *(or nori flakes)*							1 tsp.		1 tsp.
Flax meal								1 tbsp.	1 tbsp.
Hemp hearts		1 tbsp.		1 tbsp.			2 tbsp.	2 tbsp. + 1 C	1 C + 6 tbsp.
Quinoa		2 tbsp.	1 C						1 C + 2 tbsp.
Kidney beans			2 C						2 C
Lentils *(brown, dry)*		1 C							1 C
Lentils *(red, dry)*						1 & ½ C			1 & ½ C
Macadamia *(raw)*						1 cup			1 C
Maple syrup		1 tbsp.	2 tbsp. + 1 tsp.				1 tsp.	½ tsp.	3 tbsp. + 2 1/2 tsp.
Mint *(dried)*		½ tsp +							½ tsp. +
Oats *(regular, rolled)*				1 C					1 C
Oat flour								½ C	½ C
Olives				7 PC		5 PC			12 PC
Olives *(black, pitted)*					¼ C		2 tbsp.		½ C + 2 tbsp.
Olive oil		4 tbsp	2 tbsp.	2 tbsp.			4 tbsp.	1 tsp.	12 tbsp. + 1 tsp.
Orange blossom water							½ tsp.		½ tsp.
Pistachios *(raw)*	1 C								1 C
Pine nuts *(raw)*	½ C								½ C
Pine nuts			2 tbsp.						2 tbsp.
Pumpkin seeds *(unshelled)*							1 tbsp.		1 tbsp

	PREP	DAY 1	DAY 2	DAY 3	DAY 4	DAY 5	DAY 6	DAY 7	TOTAL
Raisins					1 tbsp.				**1 tbsp.**
Rosewater			1 tsp						**1 tsp.**
Sesame seeds						1 tsp.		2 tbsp.	**1 tsp + 2 tbsp.**
Brown rice Tagliatelle (package)			1						**1**
Tahini (or vegan mayonnaise)			½ C + 2 tbsp.		¼ C	1 tbsp.	2 tbsp.		**¾ C + 5 tbsp.**
Walnuts (raw)	1 C								**1 C**
Zaatar mix								1 tbsp.	**1 tbsp**

Appreciation

So many people have played a part in the creation of this book that I can never thank them all but here are a few.

My first gratitude for the teachings of Abraham and Esther Hicks which changed my life by guiding me to connect to Source and understand how the law of attraction works.

Heartfelt gratitude to the beautiful moon mother and eating psychology expert Jessica Mccleskey Hood Mahle whom I met at The Institute for Integrative Nutrition (IIN) where I got my education as a certified holistic health coach. Jessica awakened me to the power of my divine feminine and how to love my body like a goddess.

A special thank you to all my Instagram and social media "followers," my "insta family," whose constant support and appreciation kept me focused and dedicated to serve and inspire.

I am eternally grateful for all my clients. They were the first ones who demonstrated that it is possible to detoxify your mind first so that the body can follow and give sustainable results. Thank you for being a living example that the techniques in this book actually work.

A special thank you to Sally Wolfe, the editor of this book who helped me transform my ideas into a structured book and whose excitement to work on this book and encouragement were very reassuring and rewarding.

Finally, my daily gratitude goes to my family, my husband Roc, my daughters Divina and Evana, and my little baby fur Valentino for being in my life and giving the love and support needed to be of service in this world.

About the Author

Nathalie Sader is on a mission to help women awaken to their Inner Goddess and stop denying their natural instincts toward pleasure and beauty. Born and raised in Lebanon within a society that dictates how a woman should look, feel, think, and act—and where she was a practicing clinical psychologist—she has always been passionate about happiness, health, and wellness.

In the U.S. she used her talents as a health and wellness coach and plant-based chef to help her clients break through the struggle and self-loathing that keeps women tied to the obsessive and painful pursuit of the Perfect Body as the magic door to happiness and success. The heart of Nathalie's approach is both simple and powerful: Become your beautiful goddess self by choosing pleasure instead of pain, self-love instead of self-hate. In her book, she shares her personal story of how she overcame her own struggle, offering an insightful examination of our current obsessive "diet-and-detox" culture along with eight inspiring practices for awakening to a new relationship with Self, food and life. Her *7-Day Detox*, full of luscious recipes, is fittingly termed an "adventure" rather than a program.

Nathalie, the mother of two daughters who inspire her, is also a food stylist and photographer, hence the photography in this book is a labor of love. Her vision and commitment to empowering women are also celebrated in the beautiful **dress line** she has created, honoring all shapes and sizes in their uniqueness.